YEN PATH

AWAKENING YOUR HEART'S DESIRE

Published by Price World Publishing, LLC
1300 W. Belmont Ave, Suite 20G
Chicago, IL 60657

Cover & Layout Design by Raja Sekar R
Interior design consulting: Sue Balcer
Cover Logo by I Spy Design, Inc.
Editing by Jenn Sodini
Proofreading by Siobhán Gallagher
Printing by Sheridan Books

June 2011
ISBN: 978-1932549-69-0
Library of Congress Control Number: 2010932719.

Printed in the United States of America

10 9 8 7 6 5 4 3 2 1

YEN PATH

Awakening Your Heart's Desire

by
Jenny Gallagher

PRICE WORLD
PUBLISHING

CONTENTS

Introduction

The Purpose and Vision of *Yen Path*

I want to thank you for including my book in your journey. My reason for writing this book is to offer a framework for positive change. My vision is success and wellbeing for those who desire it and my purpose is to encourage and foster positive thought and action. This is an exciting time—like you, many people are ready to discover and move towards their desires. Your attitude, perceptions, beliefs, core values, and commitment will take you far in life if you use them right.

So many Americans live with extreme stress. When living with pain or struggle, including stress, it is much harder to realize your dreams. If your days are continually filled with work and responsibilities, then you may have even forgotten that you once had dreams.

Yen Path is here to offer assistance. A yen is a yearning, longing, or desire. I am a life coach and yoga teacher with a method or path, that you can follow as you reconnect with and achieve your desires. In my practice, I use yoga philosophy and life-coaching concepts to help people reduce stress and dissatisfaction, therefore improving their quality of life. I want to share this method with you.

My desired outcome for you is a renewed sense of hope as you begin to realize new possibilities. My focus is on optimism and empowerment. Many of the techniques are simple and enjoyable, so you will immediately begin to feel better. The return on investing a little effort now will be well worth it. This is a path rarely traveled, and it leads to true peace. There is no rush. Simply relax and enjoy. From here, with this book, real transformation begins. I wish you all the best.

My Personal Transformation

Years before I was a life coach or yoga teacher, I began my transformation. That may sound funny, because we all transform and change constantly. Yet there were times in my life when struggle created a significant shift for me. These shifts started with a thought—a change in my perception. I made a choice to no longer be the victim.

But I am no different from you. At many points, I have taken one step forward and two steps back. But I love life and want to make the most of it.

When I was ten years old, my family moved from warm and friendly central Florida to upstate New York. The kids were mean, and as the oldest child I felt the need to protect my siblings. As a shy, skinny little girl I had no idea how to do that. I began to feel an attraction to the "tough kids." They were cool and no one messed with them. So I made it my mission to start hanging out with them. While their company provided a feeling of acceptance, the belief that my association with them would provide protection for my siblings and me was terribly untrue. Instead, it caused nothing but turmoil in my life, and is something that I truly regret to this day. Drinking, smoking, recreational drugs, and reckless behavior took their toll on me. I literally woke up one day and decided that I needed to make some changes. I realized that the people I hung out with had no direction, and neither did I. I was fortunate; I had a strong familial support system. Even today, my parents, siblings, and I stick together. Supporting one another is our most important responsibility.

With their encouragement, I made the changes I needed to make so that I could land a good job. Shifting my focus toward a career was challenging and exciting. I moved up the corporate ladder quickly as an analyst and consultant in the field of healthcare systems development. I learned a lot and liked what I did. During my career, I was fortunate enough to work on a highly functional, empowered team (and occasionally some less functional ones). I volunteered for special projects that involved training, mentoring, team-building, and team facilitation. Understanding what motivated people was, and still is, fascinating to me. But the hours and demands created plenty of physical stress and tension with coworkers. A new transformation was occurring—one that would become crystal clear in the very near future.

In addition to the stress from work, I also struggled with physical pain from a chronic disease that prevented me from having children. At one point, I joined a support group in an attempt to gather information. In this group, I noticed that people liked to identify with pain and used it as an excuse to continue acting on their maladaptive behaviors. I realized that many people *choose* to suffer, which allowed me to make a conscious choice. I vowed not let stress or discomfort own me. On many days I have to admit failure, but self-awareness helps me to notice when I am not living with integrity. My awareness is my anchor.

Both the stress of work and the desire for increased awareness led me to start taking yoga classes. It started during an Ashtanga yoga class in 1999. I had been to other yoga classes, but this was different. After ninety minutes in this vigorous class, I realized that I spent most of the time in the present moment. Not thinking about the past or future was an amazing feeling. I was peaceful, happy, and invigorated. The high-pressure, assertive nature of my corporate world seemed unnatural. I knew that I had discovered something pretty big. Soon I realized that I wanted more than just yoga classes. I found a teacher-training program so I could learn more about it and become an instructor.

Around the same time, I met some life coaches from my women's networking group. After meeting them, I knew exactly what I wanted for my future. I had a vision and I was ready to make some changes.

In 2002, I quit my job, did some traveling, and started my first business venture. It was time to trust in this new vision and to follow it. My husband and I worked as healthcare and management consultants while I finished my coaching training. I've now been in business ever since, and love what I do.

I have been happily married for over twenty years. My husband and I share many core values, including a strong work ethic. As a matter of fact, Jody taught me to never focus on what could not be done. Together we set our dreams high.

My husband and I have relocated a lot, mostly because of his career. Relocating to a new town is challenging, but for us it's also kind of fun. I can't count the times people have asked me where we call home. Our answer is simple: It is where we are living at that moment.

I understand change, both voluntary and involuntary. You and I have had, and will continue to have, ups and downs. Through our success stories we can support each other—not only because we understand, but also because new ideas and inspiration come from sharing those stories. This is our modern-day hearth.

How to Use this Book

My method is the heart of the book and is meant to do two things: help you both think and act in a way that will create more of what you want in life. The worksheets I have developed will allow you to gain a deeper understanding about what you want. They will help you to develop a practice, or new behaviors, that will lead to positive change in your life. My method will give you step-by-step guidance.

This book will provide a variety of techniques. Pick and choose ones that will work best for you. However, I do encourage you to complete the exercises and worksheets. Make a copy of your worksheets so you can refer to your answers every day.

To support the practice worksheets, I have included concepts from the past (including ancient approaches such as Yoga teachings), the present (using life-coaching methods), and the future (by sharing scientific findings). While I am not an expert in these sciences, I want to share what I have discovered so you can understand that even the greatest minds of our time believe that changing your thoughts will change your reality.

The book is meant to be short. Some of the concepts can be a lot to absorb—like a rich dessert, sometimes a small serving is all you need. If you want to learn more, there will be some resources provided at the end of this book.

The Path

Faced with increasing demands and responsibilities, most Americans are not fulfilling their desires because they aren't sure how to fit such a pursuit into their busy schedules. Each year, the average American will work 350 hours more than the average European, in addition to spending about 100 extra hours commuting. Fifty-five percent of mothers in the United States work outside the home. Twenty-eight percent of our households are single-parent families.

"The season of failure is the best time for sowing the seeds of success."

Paramahansa Yogananda

Too many demands at work and at home create dissatisfaction and frustration, which leads to stress. In 2008, UCLA scientists found that the stress hormone cortisol suppresses the immune cells. That means stress makes people more susceptible to illness. The Centers for Disease Control (CDC) states that chronic diseases like heart disease, stroke, cancer, and diabetes are among the most prevalent, costly, and preventable of all health problems. These preventable illnesses account for eighty-three percent of total healthcare expenditures in the general population. *Yen Path* will help you manage this stress and see you through it.

This book is for you if you:

- Believe you are too busy to move forward with your desires. Recognize that this is a limiting belief and is simply not true.

- Spend so much time focused on your responsibilities that you aren't even sure what it is you desire anymore. Now is time for self-discovery.

- Have great goals and ideas but get less-than-good results. Now is the time to learn and try new things.

- Are curious and passionate about your future.

The simple and enjoyable solutions that follow will help get you started. They are a path to guide you. *Yen Path* is a holistic approach that encourages positive thought and action. If eighty-three percent of all disease is preventable, then I believe that ninety-nine percent of dissatisfaction is preventable as well. *Yen Path* will teach you how.

FORMULA FOR SUCCESS

Dissatisfaction, Frustration, or Stress →

Learn/Practice using *Yen Path* →

Fulfill Desires

Beginning Your Path: The Discovery Questionnaire

To get started, complete the Discovery Questionnaire. This will give you an idea of what desires you should focus on as you read the book.

In no time, you should start to see shifts in your life. Hopefully you will immediately benefit from the inner shifts. Focusing on what you want instead of what you do not want takes a little practice, but it will feel natural once you get the hang of it. You will feel more peaceful, relaxed, and hopeful. The bigger changes may take some time, but remember: This is a journey. Have fun with it. Love the life you are creating for yourself and love each step you take in manifesting that life.

Yen Path Worksheet:
Discovery Questionnaire

1) Rate your overall satisfaction level in the
following areas
1 = low, 2 = medium, 3 = high

_____ Career/School
_____ Finances
_____ Health
_____ Significant Other
_____ Family life
_____ Friends (list each separately)
_____ Community
_____ Physical Environment/Home
_____ Other (list each separately)

2) From the categories above that rated the
lowest answer the following questions:

   A. Can you clearly articulate your
desires? If yes, then write each here
or on the back.

B. If your answer to A is no, can you identify how you would like to feel, look, think, etc.? If yes, then list whatever comes to mind.

C. If your answer to B is no, then first list how you currently feel, look, think, etc. Then look at the words you used and write down words that are the exact opposite (e.g., feel sad → feel happy; out of shape → healthy; worry about finances → in control of finances; broke → rich; lonely → popular)

3) Have you been unsuccessful with past attempts to achieve your desires? If so, list what you have tried to do. Read the remaining chapters and then come up with a totally new approach.

4) Do you want to learn techniques to help you center and create clarity? If yes, then read Chapter Two.

5) Do you want to learn more about life balance? If yes, then read Chapter Three.

6) Do you want to learn how to develop an action plan? If yes, then read Chapter Four.

7) Are you ready to expand your horizons? If yes, then read Chapter Five.

8) Are you ready to relax and read some stories? If yes, then read Chapter Six.

How *Yen Path* Helps You Manage Stress

The Oxford American Dictionary defines stress as tension. In physics, tension is "stress produced by forces pulling apart." For humans, these forces can be emotional or physical, actual or perceived.

Millions of people are struggling with the side effects of a fast-paced lifestyle. In addition, people face added stress from the past recession, or an economic "exhale," which adds fear and uncertainty. The misconception that things should always expand or grow is as ridiculous as imagining that we can simply continue to breathe inward. Yet, with this exhale comes pain. It's important for us to define stress, understand stress at a biological level, and see the benefits of stress. From here we can then distinguish what stress is necessary and what is not, and manage it more easily.

We have physiological responses to stress. One response is commonly known as "fight or flight." When this occurs, hormones are released that divert blood to all the systems of the body that will assist in either fight or flight. Muscles tense, eyes dilate, and breath shortens, among other physical reactions.

But our body also has a "rest and digest" response. One way it is activated is through full, comfortable breathing. This technique improves the immune system and digestion, and allows the body to restore and rejuvenate. Chapter Two discusses centering, and many of its techniques will allow you to create a relaxing internal environment.

There are a wide range of responses to your relative stress and relaxation. It's important to understand that neither response is simply "good" or "bad." Stress can be good while relaxation can be boring and un-motivating at times. If we did not have some level of stress response, we'd have a hard time feeling awake and alert. Without these stress hormones, it would be hard to be creative, adventurous, or passionate about life. Dr. Hans Selye wrote several books based on his stress research. He classifies stress into two categories: eustress and distress. Eustress is considered healthy stress, while distress leads to anxiety and depression. It is important to notice which type of stress you are feeling and then learn how to harness this energy. Use it wisely, and you will be productive and feel good. That means knowing when to slow down so that you can build-in quality rest and restoration.

You will find ideas for achieving this goal in Chapter Two.

In many situations, however, stress is a response to an imagined threat. This concept is helpful when thinking about making life changes. Many people will choose to not make positive life changes because the idea of change stirs up fear and anxiety. These are common feelings and can be approached in many ways. First, examine the thoughts and feelings you have about a situation. You rarely need to act before you are ready. And if you shift your perspective on change, you may find it begins naturally.

For example, consider the latest recession. When you hear the word *recession* a perception forms in your mind. When we examine this perception, we find it creates a feeling, and that feeling is what may lead us to respond in a certain way. Therefore, if you want to change the feeling, you need to change the thought.

EXERCISE 1.1:
Identifying and Shifting Perspective

1. *Write down your thoughts (perceptions) about the word* **recession**, *or any other word you are currently struggling with.*

2. *Write down how these thoughts make you feel.*

3. *Write down how you respond to, or act in response to, the perceptions and feelings.*

4. *Write down words, feelings, and actions that would be the exact opposite of recession.*

CAN YOU SHIFT YOUR PERSPECTIVE TO MOTIVATE YOU INSTEAD OF STALL YOU?

When you thought of the word *recession*, did you have negative thoughts and feelings and recognize some fear-based actions? When people are afraid, they tend to move into a holding pattern, kind of like a deer frozen in the headlights. Instead, learn how to enjoy the simple things in life and connect with feelings of happiness, contentment, and gratitude. Be excited about possibilities and how you can improve your quality of life. Look at the positive aspects of a required change, like how being frugal helps you learn new skills and value money. Use the previous exercise when you feel stuck or scared to see if there is a better way of thinking about your current, tough issue.

Dr. Robert Heller said, "Fear is excitement without breath." For now, consider this quote and know that a distinction can be made between fear and excitement—especially when you're considering making a life change. So take a few deep breaths and try to find the excitement around your desires.

A Holistic Approach

What is a holistic approach? Yoga, *Ayurveda* (the sister science to yoga), and traditional Chinese medicine are holistic approaches. This means that the focus is on the whole person, using body and mind integration, instead of treating the illness or problem (also known as the allopathic approach) as a strictly physical issue. Both approaches are valuable, but since yoga and life coaching focus on integration instead of segregation, so will this book.

Positive life change is best achieved when you shift your focus from the source of your pain to what is desired. While pain can be a great motivator for change, a different perspective is needed for you to feel complete and capable instead of incomplete or a victim of circumstance. This is a powerful starting point.

EXERCISE 1.2

Close your eyes and see yourself as perfect in this moment—not in the future or in the past, but right now. Say, in your heart, that all is well and make this your reality. Begin to feel the effect.

Notice how the tension leaves your body. Let your jaw and facial muscles relax. Relax your shoulders and your hands. Feel your breath. This moment is perfect and simple.

Start here, at perfection. Now you are ready for your journey. Imagine the path that lies ahead of you, with all its promise and hope. Trust in yourself as you move toward the possibilities that are waiting for you.

Life coaching is a holistic approach that helps you focus on what is desirable. Life coaches will help you focus on the big picture (the wholeness of your life). Having a vision is necessary for creating goals that will produce favorable results. Done this way, you may also find that you connect to your life purpose and undergo transformation. When you align with your true purpose you are on the right path, and you will know it. This may also lead you to what is known as *Dharma*, which means "right action" and describes any virtuous path.

Advantages to Dissatisfaction

Life coaches use a term called *reframing*. Reframing allows you to look at something from a different perspective, just as you did in Exercise 1.1. Here are some opportunities to look at the positive side to dissatisfaction. Sound strange? Read on, and you'll see how even something negative—like dissatisfaction—can benefit you.

Motivation

There are different forms of motivation, but essentially motivation is the drive to move toward something desirable and away from something that is undesirable; therefore, dissatisfaction is a motivator. Dissatisfaction is a form of pain that alerts you to a problem. If the problem is significant, the action is immediate and rarely pondered. Little deliberation is needed before moving aside as a car races toward you. When problems aren't as severe, or when the situation is complicated, thought is required in order to determine the best course of action. The Strategizing Worksheet in Chapter Four can help in these situations.

Before we move forward, let's make a distinction about dissatisfaction. Some dissatisfaction arises from a current circumstance, and another type arises from the discomfort of trying something new. This latter kind can stop you in your tracks and hold you back from achieving your goals. When trying something new, pay attention to the new sensations—if they are mild feelings of dissatisfaction, ignore them and stick with your plan. It takes courage to be around new people and to learn and do new things.

Let's use an example: You have been dissatisfied with the lack of exercise you are getting, so you decide to join a gym. Your motivation is high as you step onto the treadmill or into your first aerobics or yoga class. Ideally, you would no longer feel dissatisfaction, sure that you had made the right decision. Continuing would be easy. While this occasionally does happen, this is not the experience for most of us.

Unfortunately, this experience is often one that produces a new form of dissatisfaction. It may just be that you feel out of place, or it may be that you feel like the exercise is too challenging for you. Sound familiar? Instead of dropping out, remind yourself to interpret the new information. First, make sure that you are safe. If you are at no risk of injury, then stay with the challenge and understand that the activity will get easier with practice. Before you know it, you will begin to enjoy yourself. Just know it doesn't always happen on day one.

Here's another example: Your dissatisfaction is loneliness, but you are either shy or not sure how to meet new people. If you are simply not sure how to meet people and then finally find a way to do so, you may easily achieve your goal. However, if you are shy, the fear of meeting people may also be a fear of change—which means that getting out and meeting people is probably the exact right thing to do. Aligning with your desire sometimes means taking a small risk and feeling a bit uncomfortable at first. Just like the aerobics class, it may feel odd and awkward a few times, but this temporary dissatisfaction should not motivate you to stop doing what is an otherwise right action. In short, a new behavior feels strange at first, but you shouldn't mistake that strangeness for dissatisfaction and pain. A shy person can begin to achieve immediate results by simply shifting the thought from "being alone" or "being shy" to warmer ones, like "being happy."

Information

New experiences help you learn more about yourself. It is possible that you'll try something and hate it. That's OK—you are experimenting. Do not interpret the disappointments as failures and give up. Instead, you can set a new course of action and find something better suited to you.

For example, you may have tried dozens of diets without success. That doesn't mean you are a failure; it simply means you have not found a technique that is right for you. Most diets fail because people focus on deprivation and willpower, and neither focus will produce good long-term results. Later in this book, we will talk about nutrition and fitness, because the only way to have enough energy to achieve your goals is to feel good.

What if you have great goals but have been getting poor results? You may need more clarity around your goal, which will produce different actions altogether.

Shifting Perspective

Yen Path helps you to get immediate results by shifting your perception. Sometimes the correct action is to first observe your thoughts to see if a mental shift is required. Are you simply drawn to focusing on a tired muscle, an awkward moment, how little time and money you have, or how unhappy you are? Can you instead bring your attention to your desires and your goals?

If you are staying with dissatisfaction because of fear or uncertainty, then maybe you are not ready—and that is fine. Use this book to do an inner exploration to gain information before you try to shift your perspective. Before you know it, you may be ready to move into action. A life coach can also help you explore your goals and possibilities.

Yoga and Life Coaching Similarities

Following are examples of problematic situations and explanations as to how they can be tackled by both life coaching and yoga. These are just a few of the many issues that can be addressed by both disciplines, but these examples will provide a good starting point to help you understand the *Yen Path* approach. When you feel frustrated about something, try something new. Refer to the topics below for some ways to look at your situation with a new perspective.

The table will help you see how different teachings can relate to the topics that will be covered in this book. You will find more details about each topic and the related concepts in the pages that follow.

Topic	Yoga Approach	Life Coaching Approach
Self-deception	Maya (Illusion)	Meeting Needs, False Belief
Identifying Obstacles	Patanjali's Nine Obstacles	Maslow's Hierarchy of Needs
Identifying Your Desires	Mantra, 6th Limb (Concentration)	Creating a Vision
Support	Gatherings	Mastermind Group
Achieving Your Goals	Dharma (Right Action)	Life Purpose, Action Plan

1. Self-Deception

Do you remember a time in your life when all of a sudden you realized you were wrong about something? You've probably have had an argument with someone and then admitted you were wrong. Most of us have learned something new that changed our beliefs at various points in our lives. But sometimes these self-deceptions are hard to see, even with the best of intentions.

For example, maybe you always thought you were helping someone out, when in fact you were not giving him a chance to try something independently—your wish to nurture him actually prevented his growth, but you couldn't see past your desire to nurture. Did you self-examine this need to nurture? Was it self-motivated in any way? Maybe you help others to feel important or needed. If you are trying to justify your actions, then see the situation as an opportunity for self-examination. Taking time to understand yourself will free you from these self-deceptions and will allow you to act from a place of keen awareness about the impact of your actions on yourself and others. If you are unhappy, then consider getting to the root cause so you can move forward.

" True yoga is not about the shape of your body, but the shape of your life. Yoga is not to be performed; yoga is to be lived. Yoga doesn't care about what you have been; yoga cares about the person you are becoming. "

Aadil Palkhivala

The Yogic Concept of Maya

Every experience and thought is filtered through your mind. Therefore, your thoughts create your reality. The filtering uses information from past experiences, what you were taught, and how you feel. Because of the filtering process, a person's reality is in fact more of a perception, and it can be flawed. The ancient Yogic teachings call these illusions maya. It is believed that maya, or these illusions, creates all suffering.

An example of a Yogic maya is the idea that we are all separate. Yoga teaches us that this idea of separation is an illusion; we are, in fact, part of a whole. Yogic teaching espouses that you can honor someone without agreeing with them. Acting as if we are separate from each other creates conflict among us. Peace begets peace.

You do not need to believe in this Yogic teaching of "oneness" in order to take away something very meaningful here. If you examine the concept of oneness, you will benefit in many ways. You will not feel isolated or alone. You may discover that a person you struggle with is not so different from yourself. Even if you are arguing opposite sides of a debate, you may discover that you are both passionate about what you believe in. Any time you are struggling with a situation, consider all sides. Are you honoring others? If you talk behind someone's back or withhold information from others, then you may want to consider why. Address the hidden fears to unravel the illusion you have created. This is a great approach to help you with forgiveness. At times we all struggle with forgiving both others and ourselves.

False Beliefs

Coaches work with clients to identify the client's false beliefs and unmet needs, and how to best respond to them. Not all needs are basic like food and water. When these less-obvious needs go unsatisfied, they can create a hunger so distracting that it is impossible for you to achieve anything else.

Consider the example of "nurturing" used above. Most of us believe that the desire to nurture is good. However, you may nurture someone even if it is not good for him. Yet because you have such a strong belief about nurturing, you may continue to do it even if it causes more harm. If the action of nurturing is causing more harm than good, you must examine and change this belief. If you nurture someone to feel needed, are you enabling a bad behavior? Do you feel taken advantage of? Is the other person is lacking in certain skills like thoughtfulness? Life coaches work with clients to cut through some of these beliefs and uncover the real motivations and desires. By considering your beliefs, you may discover ways to kindly and compassionately change your actions.

Identifying Obstacles

Sometimes problems must be resolved before moving toward your desires. It is important to identify and examine these obstacles, both the internal and external ones.

Patanjali's Nine Obstacles

Patanjali wrote about removing obstacles in the Yoga Sutras over 2000 years ago. He described the nine obstacles as illness, lethargy, doubt, haste or impatience, resignation or fatigue, distraction, ignorance or arrogance, inability to take a new step, and loss of confidence. When these obstacles are present, achieving your goals is much harder. In yoga, we examine and identify these obstacles, both in the physical practice of yoga and in our own lives.

Maslow's Hierarchy of Needs

Just as a yoga instructor helps participants, life coaches also work with clients to identify obstacles. This ties into the earlier discussion of false beliefs and unmet needs; often our internal obstacles signify a greater need. One rubric life coaches use to identify these unmet needs and subsequent obstacles was created in 1943 by Abraham Maslow. In his book *A Theory of Human Motivation*, Maslow describes a hierarchy of needs, explaining that physiological, safety, love, belonging, and esteem needs must be satisfied for a person to progress to the highest achievement of self-actualization. He established his findings by studying the healthiest and most motivated college students, and his work has brought the idea of the importance of personal development into psychology, academics, and business. These unmet needs are obstacles themselves. Just as in yoga, these obstacles can be present internally and externally. Life coaches work with you to help you fill these internal and external needs.

This is not to say that all external obstacles can be removed with yoga or life coaching. It is essential to recognize real-world stressors. While internal, mental, and emotional work can be done around these issues, it is important to remember that some things cannot be solved with self-examination alone. Do not think that the presence of obstacles represents a failure of your self-study. It is OK to take a break from working on long-term goals and improvement to deal with especially tough issues in life. And know that you don't have to work on obstacles alone. Call upon friends, family, support groups, and professionals to help you along the way.

Identifying Your Desires

Can you see what you want, or do you focus on the struggle? If you are having trouble identifying your desires and goals, you can use both Yogic and life-coaching techniques to help you get the calm and focus you need to identify your desires. Sometimes people get so wrapped up in the chaos of life and in the actions of "doing" that they don't stop to figure out what they want.

The Sixth Limb of Yoga (Concentration) and Mantra

In Patanjali's descriptions of the eight limbs of Yoga, only one limb relates to the postures. Another important teaching is that of concentration, and that is the sixth limb of Yoga. One must learn to concentrate before one can learn to meditate. Many people find it is easiest to quiet the mind by focusing on one thing. You can focus on something physical like your breath, or something you create using your imagination, like a flower. One-mindedness allows you to concentrate on one thing, which prevents the mind from wandering all over the place.

This is often a case when yoga practitioners will use a *mantra*, which a repeated word, prayer, or idea, to focus on. Yogis believe powerful transformation can come from a mantra. It can be said aloud or repeated in the mind. The words can have significance, but do not need it. Simply repeating an arbitrary word allows you to concentrate and quiet the mind. However, selecting a word with meaning can have a profound impact.

If you are new to the idea, in Chapter Two there is a practice meditation technique using the mantra "I am."

Creating a Vision

Because it is so easy for people to focus on the pain in their life, it is therefore easy for that pain to become a mantra of sorts. Life coaches try to see through these ruminations and help you shift focus onto a vision that you create. It is an essential first step. This book heavily focuses on techniques for creating a vision.

Support

Yoga philosophy and life coaching also intersect at the concept of support, or *satsang*. Our society has placed value on being independent, and independence does have its advantages. But have you ever noticed that successful people surround themselves with successful people? You don't need a lot of money to do this. Get a mastermind partner or find people with similar interests, and then team up. Each of us has different strengths and experiences that we can benefit from. Create your own board of directors and watch your investments (in yourself) grow.

Achieving Your Goals

Dharma

In Yoga philosophy, Dharma is used to describe one's righteous duty or virtuous path. This path is what many begin to discover through the self-actualization process. That does not imply a rigid, direct correlation—a person seeking self-development may be surprised where they end up. Life coaches help clients to make sure that they are on the right path before creating an action plan. Knowing who you are and what you want is an important first step. This will save time, money, and frustration. Real-world strategies for finding your life's purpose and setting up an action plan—those "right actions"—are explored in detail in this book.

Center

B y the end of this chapter you will have greater clarity about your desires. This chapter addresses the idea of "centering." Only when you are centered and grounded will you have the roots that will support positive change.

" If you do what you've always done, you'll get what you've always gotten. "

Tony Robbins

One element of centering requires a reduction of mental clutter. It's impossible to find the center of anything if it is disorganized and chaotic. More importantly, you need to make space in your head for the thoughts that will be part of the new you. You would never redecorate the living room with the old stuff still inside it; you would empty the room and clean it first. We will explore the nature of thoughts and how they can clutter and even conflict within your own mind. Then we will explore focusing and meditation exercises that will help you calm the chaos and resolve the conflicts.

Once you have some "space," then you must understand your identity and your core values. You can make space for a center, but you cannot leave it empty. We will explore both what makes up your "center" and, if you want to change it, what the new one might look like.

The Anatomy of a Thought

The average person has approximately 60,000 thoughts a day, most of which are not original. In other words, you have thought them over and over again. Thought patterns are habitual. If you want to create a good foundation for positive growth, you must first understand how thoughts work and where they originate. These repetitive thoughts are called ruminations, and they create strong neural pathways.

For our purposes, all that matters are those ruminations that are preventing good results or outcomes. Here is an opportunity to explore these thoughts in a new way.

This book will explore the three strong energetic centers in the body that relate to thought. Below are some of the characteristics of the three centers that thoughts and feelings originate from. Use this information to understand how you think, and analyze whether your thought habits are serving you well. If not, know you can change the way you think about things. It just takes practice.

Heart (Feeling Center)

The physical heart is part of the cardiovascular system. However, it is important to analyze the heart in a more abstract way. We will discuss *chakras* later, but know now that the heart chakra is considered the energy center. If you have ever had a broken heart then you know that you feel it in your chest; it can feel like your heart is literally breaking. Envy, jealousy, and hatred are feelings that words can barely describe. We also feel love and joy in the heart center. If you see something beautiful or funny, you can feel it in your chest. Feelings can be rich, intense, and raw. They can be all-consuming, and in certain situations, like the death of a loved one, this is to be expected. However, if emotions seem to continually control your environment, if you are always giving to others and never caring for yourself, or if you are unable to feel compassion, it is likely you have an imbalance in the heart center.

Gut (Instinct)

The stomach has nerve cells that secrete neurotransmitters. In fact, it is sometimes called the "second brain." In terms of chakras, this is the center of creativity. It is also somewhat of a "dumping ground" for unprocessed emotion. As you will learn later in the Ayurveda overview, everything we input must be digested, processed, or assimilated. When emotions such as fear, guilt, and shame cannot be processed, they are stored in the lower three chakras. An explanation of what that means will be provided later. For now, understand that it is extremely important to understand your feelings and to rid yourself of negative energy.

Head (Brain, Mind, and Ego)

The brain processes input signals from both the outside environment (using sight, sound, touch, taste, and smell) and our internal environment (the conscious and subconscious mind). The conscious mind does the thinking and observing. The subconscious mind is all of your preprogramming. If you dislike something but aren't sure why, then the subconscious mind is at work.

Neural pathways travel through the nervous system and interpret these impulses. Once an interpretation has occurred, it is likely that it will occur again and again; in other words, the thought will repeat itself. For example, if you were listening to a song when someone broke up with you, it is likely that when you hear the song in the future it will remind you of that moment. If we experience a trauma, like being called a name, that thought will frequently come to mind. But you can change that, either through practice on your own or through cognitive behavioral therapy, which is a type of psychotherapy that helps clients overcome unwanted thinking patterns and make changes to the subconscious mind.

Psychoanalysis refers to something called the "ego." The word is often used to describe arrogance or an overinflated sense of self, but that is not how we are using the term here. In this discussion, the ego is the part of the psyche that separates 'self' from 'non-self.' It is the part of us that self-identifies—it's how we label ourselves. But there are risks when you identify too strongly with your own labels. Before moving on, let's take a moment to discuss how the ego works.

The ego is essential to your function, but it can also be a dangerous weapon. The ego can self-inflate, self-deprecate, judge, distort, and label. It's that voice inside your head that never seems to rest. Having a strong sense of self is very different than feeding your ego. The ego is never satisfied and will always want your undivided attention. The ego is not bad; it simply needs to be monitored. A person that is too self-centered, either because of pride or insecurity, has an imbalance in this energetic center.

"Wisdom is knowing I am nothing. Love is knowing I am everything and between the two my life moves."

Nisargadatta Maharaj

Because we define ourselves with the ego, it will often create self-centered needs. That same mechanism can also cause negative self-labeling. You are self-labeling when you have a thought that starts with "I am," "I always," or "I do." Some of the labels are fine and can actually be part your core values, such as "I enjoy spending time with my family." But we run into trouble when we create a false identity from mislabeling.

Here is an example: Let's say you see a television commercial for a luxury car or an expensive piece of jewelry. The commercial conveys a sense of elegance that you desire. Ask yourself, "Do I want the car or that feeling?" If it is the feeling, then ask yourself, "If I own the car, will that make me elegant?" You might say "yes," but that doesn't make it true. The most elegant car does not make an aggressive driver, always honking the horn and yelling at people, an elegant person.

The television commercial implies elegance, and your ego processes that association and creates that label, but elegant *actions* are required to make elegance a reality. If labels can be false, then your self-image may be as well. If you think you are elegant and the people around you do not, then your self-awareness may be off.

Because identity is so intrinsic to ego, we often feel defensive when our ego is challenged. But if you defend your position all the time, you may not realize that you're defending and reinforcing something that might be false. When feelings like defensiveness, anger, or jealousy occur, it is very likely that your ego is involved. Take a moment to notice what triggered the feeling and enjoy a few steady breaths. Keep a cool head so you can move forward in a productive manner. Not working so hard to defend the ego can reduce a lot of tension in your life.

When your ego feels threatened, use the exercises in this chapter to quiet it. Taking time to learn about yourself and to create true self-awareness is critical to your success. You will break through misconceptions and be a much better person for it. From here, true progress and success can be achieved.

Reconciling Conflicting Inputs

If you have ever experienced a situation in which you have come up with a resolution to a problem only to find you cannot sleep at night, then you have experienced these forces described previously working against each other. The conflict arises when there is a hidden truth you are ignoring for one reason or another. Be very careful to move along a path that will satisfy your goals and allow you to remain in integrity with yourself and others.

Let's say you are unhappy at work. You want to quit your job and travel around the world. You wish you had done so after college, but you got married and started a family instead. You know that if you tell your wife about your plan, then she will be angry. Now you begin to feel resentment. You are mad at your wife because of thoughts you have created.

Any thought that makes you feel anxious, angry, jealous, fearful, or insecure is your body's alarm telling you that it is time to pay attention to conflicting signals from within. This does not mean you need to give up your dreams. Through clarity and planning you can figure out how to fit your goals into your life and remain in integrity.

Remember that you have established habitual thought patterns, which will produce habitual actions. If you want real change in your life, consider taking time to think differently. One way of doing this is to imagine you are someone you admire. How would they handle the situation? Then try that action and see what new results you get.

Clearing the Mental Clutter

The internal conflict of thoughts and feelings described above is mental clutter. To sort through these conflicts, you must create some space amid that clutter.

Yoga practitioners have used concentration, meditation, and *pranayama* (breathing practices) for millennia to deal with this issue and "create space." Concentration and meditation both help to create a sense of clarity.

The untrained mind simply runs from thought to thought, which makes it hard to focus. Many times these thoughts even contradict each other. In one thought you may feel confident, and then in the very next thought you will put yourself down for feeling that way. Concentrating on one thought with intention removes the clutter, or what Yogis refer to as "monkey mind." When you observe monkeys jumping from tree to tree, it is easy to understand the similarity to our thoughts—the ones that hop about with seemingly no rhyme or reason. Instead, learn how to focus your thoughts on what you want to create. You will find this to be very powerful in the manifestation of your desires.

While concentration focuses the mind, it is meditation that quiets it. Just think about how hard it is to concentrate on something, like reading, with lots of loud distraction

EXERCISE 2.1:
Releasing Thought

Imagine each thought is a ripple in what otherwise would be a still body of water. If the surface has ripples from movement, it is not possible to see what is beneath. The same is true when you are trying to create a deeper understanding about you and your desires. You must first disengage from repetitious thoughts in order to explore deeper.

Close your eyes. Every time a thought presents itself, see the ripple and release the thought. It is your choice to engage in the thought or to simply let it pass. When you choose to release, you may begin to notice a feeling of relaxation. Self-discovery is possible in these quiet moments.

around. To achieve internal focus, you need internal quiet. Meditation is the gap between the thoughts. It's the space and silence in between. With practice, the gap can increase, leaving a peaceful and clear mind.

Clearing the Physical Clutter

We will explore physical health later in this book, but it is important to note that physical clutter—both in your environment and within your own body—will interfere with your ability to clear mental clutter. You know how you feel if you overeat or have too much coffee? Concentration becomes difficult because you either feel tired or wired. You have an over-accumulation of something, which has the same impact as an over-cluttered garage or office. Your energy drains from the excess. It's easy to manage small amounts of things like fatigue, stress, and depression, but over-accumulation will cause the problems.

Nourishment, hydration, rest, exercise, cleanliness, and good general self-care are critical to helping you focus and clear mental clutter, which will in turn help you achieve your dreams.

Practice Listening: Meditation Exercises

When the mind stops talking at you, you can finally listen. This is necessary for centering. You will learn more about yourself in many ways, including distinguishing false labels from core values. You will begin to uncover what is truly important to you so that you can come up with an action plan. If you create goals before taking time to learn about yourself, then you will just waste your time and money. Use the following exercises to practice listening.

Rhythmic Breathing

Rhythmic breathing helps to calm you. Have you ever heard you should breathe into a paper bag if you are hyperventilating? Really you don't need the bag. What you need is to focus on breathing and not the anxiety in your mind.

**EXERCISE 2.2:
Rhythmic Breathing**

Try this practice for one minute.

- *Bring your attention to your breath. If your breath seems shallow or short, then lengthen your breath. These changes should feel relaxing and peaceful, not forced.*

- *Notice the rhythm of your breath. It should be soothing, like that of a rocking chair.*

- *Notice the sound of your breath. It should be soft, like the sound of gentle waves.*

- *Notice the temperature of the air as it travels into the nostrils.*

- *Notice the temperature of the air as it travels out of the nostrils.*

The Body Scan: Yoga-Nidra

Yoga-nidra means "yogic sleep." Resting in a conscious state is rejuvenating for the body and the mind. You can use this method to focus on anything that is calming. However, this exercise illustrates its use through the body scan.

EXERCISE 2.3:
Yoga-Nidrausing The Body Scan

- *Start with a few rounds of rhythmic breathing to allow the body and mind to settle.*

- *Bring your attention to your navel center and envision a beautiful glowing light deep inside the abdomen.*

- *Believe with your heart that this is a healing light and that every place the light touches is cleansed and purified.*

- *Let the light begin to expand and fill the abdomen.*

- *Move the light throughout every section of your torso—front to back, side to side.*

- *See the light travel down into the hips, legs, feet, and toes.*

- *See the light travel into the shoulders and down the arms into the hands and fingers.*

- *Move the light up the neck and into the head, face, and skull.*

- *See yourself resting in this cleansed and purified state for as long as you wish.*

Mantra

A mantra is simply a thought that you can focus on. If you do not wish to use this specific mantra, then try anything you like. It can be a word that has great meaning for you or a random word. At the very least, it allows the mind to focus on one thing. This eliminates mind chatter, which is relaxing. If the word has great meaning for you, then your mantra is even more powerful because you are focusing on a desire. Deepak Chopra suggests using the mantra of "I am" because it is a thought with no history.

EXERCISE 2.4:
The "I am" mantra

You can do this while seated, standing, lying down, or on a peaceful walk.

- *As you inhale, say the word "I" quietly to yourself.*

- *As you exhale, say the word "am" quietly to yourself.*

- *Repeat for at least three minutes*

Contemplation

Contemplation can be a form of meditation or prayer, but it does not need to be. Quality observance of an object can allow for a deep, inner connection and a greater understanding of both yourself and the world around you. From here intentions can manifest.

**EXERCISE 2.5:
Contemplation**

- *Find a short reading or beautiful piece of art, scenery or music to enjoy.*

- *Contemplate the meaning of the words or sensations.*

- *Do this for at least three minutes.*

Creating a Healthy Identity

Now that you have some skills to help you quiet the mind and sort through internal conflicts, it is important to examine what you understand to be your identity. It's time to challenge the ego.

Before you create your vision, simply take a moment to ask yourself "Who am I?" It helps to know who you are (or you who think you are) before you decide where you want to go. If you were going on a trip, your vision would be your destination and your mission would be your travel plans. But it is your purpose that drives all of it. All of these can and will change throughout your lifetime. Creating a healthy identity will allow you to understand yourself so you can better align your vision, mission, purpose, and goals.

A healthy identity is one that is much more than labels, which are so common in our society. For example, when you meet someone for the first time, the first question is often "What do you do?" We do this because of our own attachment to labels. This kind of question is fine unless we never go any deeper than the label. This does not mean that you should share intimate details with someone that you just met. But you should challenge yourself to answer the question "Who am I?" without referring to yourself with superficial labels. If you are struggling with this, try the following exercise.

EXERCISE 2.6:
My Good Qualities

- *Make a list of your good qualities.Don't leave anything out.*

- *Make a list of things you do that you enjoy.*

- *Examine your less-than-good qualities and reframe them into something positive.For example, if you anger easily, is it because you are passionate?*

CREATING AWARENESS AROUND A GOOD QUALITY LIKE PASSION CAN ALLOW YOU TO ACT IN A WAY THAT SHOWS INTEREST AND UNDERSTANDING, THUS REDUCING THE NEED TO REACT WITH ANGER OR FRUSTRATION.

Your passions and positive qualities will lead you to your purpose. We will work on creating a purpose statement later. For now, create an identity that is multifaceted and connects with the real you. A healthy identity does not come from a place of pride or hubris. A healthy identity allows you to feel comfortable with yourself.

Core Values

Understanding your core values will also help you learn more about yourself. When you value something, you hold it in the highest regard. You may value lots of things, but your core values are those things that really make you tick. If you have strong family values, many of your actions will revolve around family. If you strongly value achievement or adventure, your family may take a back seat.

You may value accuracy and always strive for perfection. You may value beauty and enjoy visiting art museums. You may value generosity, honesty, humor, independence, integrity, love, or money. You may value personal growth or prestige. You may value trust, wellness, and peace. These are just some examples of many types of core values.

While many of us share similar core values, what makes us unique is the order of importance for each; we all have a hierarchy. Taking time to understand your most important core values is helpful because you will probably include some of this information in your vision, mission, and purpose statements. This is what makes you who you are. If you are not sure what your core values are, take some time to think about it. When you are unable to live in accordance with one of your core values, you will surely feel the dissonance.

If you value independence, but someone you love has been exceptionally clingy lately, then you may start to feel anxious. Or if you value trust and someone you care for has lied to you, then you may feel extremely hurt. These feelings will introduce you to your core values.

It is important to note that the dissonance you feel when living out of alignment with a core value may leave you wondering if you are dealing with a wounded ego. Take time to examine what you are feeling and create the distinction. A wounded ego can be ignored. However, you want to take steps to live in alignment with your core values.

The Benefits of a Clear Intention

After you learn to quiet the mind chatter and learn more about yourself, you can begin to create what you want. Now it is time to create an intention. This does not mean a specific goal; we'll work on goals later. For now you should be vague. Think abstractly. Focus on a general path that you want to follow. Later you will learn how to travel down that path. Here are a few benefits of having a clear intention:

1. **You're not focusing on pain, frustration, or dissatisfaction.** It's easy to get stuck in these feelings; they grab your attention. But you don't need to stay there. You have the power to shift your attention. Doing so will move you forward. Not doing so will

keep you stuck, which adds stress to the equation.

2. **Knowing what you want is the first step to success.** Here's an example: Let's say someone at work has just told you that a coworker got an unexpected promotion. Your initial reaction is that you wish it was you who got the promotion. Just a few moments ago, this thought never crossed your mind. Here you have a choice: You can be angry and resentful, or you can realize you now have a new intention and start to consider the steps you need to take to get yourself there.

3. **You are more likely to get what you want.** Understanding your desires allows you to align your actions with them. If you believe you have been

doing exceptional work in your current position, you may decide to schedule a meeting with your boss to share these facts. You can also ask your boss what it is you need to do to move to the next level and then start working on improvements in those areas.

4. **You are less likely to feel jealous of others because you will be happy with yourself.** A person with clear intentions has a focus. You are less likely to want to use your time focusing on negative feelings. If something does occur that points out a desire you were unaware of, you can begin creating your goal and action plan.

Balance

This chapter defines and discusses life balance and compares it to techniques required for maintaining physical balance. Life balance is not about spending the same amount of time focusing on the main life categories (refer to the Discovery Questionnaire for a complete listing). Life balance is about making the most out of life. Avoiding unnecessary life struggles will allow you to move forward with efficiency. Life balance allows you to continue to grow and to move towards your desires.

Life balance comes from awareness. This allows you to notice when a shift is occurring so that you can make minor adjustments. If you wait until the dissatisfaction is significant, it is more likely that a major upheaval will occur. This chapter will teach you how to improve your balance and awareness. As Michael Singer says in his book *The Untethered Soul*:

" All the great teachings reveal the way of the center, the way of balance. Constantly look to see if that's where you are living or if you are lost in the extremes. The extremes create their opposites; the wise avoid them. Find the balance in the center and you will live in harmony. "

What is Life Balance?

One definition of balance is a sense of harmony, satisfaction, or ease. If you feel at ease, then most likely you do not need to expend any effort in creating change. However, most of us feel uneasy in some way. Many of us focus too much on one or two specific areas of our lives. While you may need to focus most of your energy on your career, school, or family, you don't want to completely ignore the other areas. If you're having trouble identifying imbalances, you should refer to the Discovery Questionnaire in Chapter One. Take note of your dissatisfaction and the dissatisfaction of those around you. This awareness can be your guide for identifying a life imbalance.

" The power of unfulfilled desires is the root of all man's slavery. "

Paramahansa Yogananda

Comparing life balance to physical balance will help us understand this concept. Most of us are so good at standing that we don't even realize the balance and coordination required to do so. If all of a sudden you were not able to balance easily on your two feet, like if you were on a boat in rough seas, you would have to concentrate on walking much more than you normally would. Life imbalance draws away our attention, pulls our mind in a direction, and makes us work so much harder in other areas of our life.

Try standing on one leg. You will become acutely aware of a physical shift that happens to keep you upright. Any shift to the left will require a counter shift to the right. If the shifts are small, then you will remain upright. If a shift in one direction is too great, then the imbalance will require you to set the other foot back on the ground.

In life, a minor dissatisfaction or imbalance is manageable. Let's say you're hungry; you eat and then you feel better and stop thinking about food. Or maybe you miss a friend; in this case you are likely to give them a call. But what if you believe you are too busy to take time to eat a nourishing meal or to call your friend? If it's only temporary, or if you only neglect those things occasionally, then it probably won't matter. But if ignoring your instincts becomes a habit, and you continually grab a candy bar or ignore your need for friendship, you may begin to notice greater imbalances that cannot be resolved with a quick readjustment. All of a sudden you realize you have twenty pounds to lose and no friends to call. If imbalance (dissatisfaction) is ignored, then the condition will worsen. Please keep in mind that the purpose of examining balance is not to compel you, in an attempt to correct imbalance, to neglect your primary responsibilities. The purpose is to give you permission to examine your feelings so that you can come up with a reasonable action plan.

Start this examination process by completing the Balancing Worksheet that follows. Review the questions at the beginning of the remaining sections, and if something rings true to you, then consider if there is an opportunity to bring about positive change.

Sometimes self-discovery can be exciting and motivating, but sometimes the opposite can happen. Know that it is fine if you discover something you are not ready to change. If you are not sure what or how to change, then keep reading. For now, you only need to create awareness that you desire change.

Using Opposites to Find the Center

Our minds like to categorize information, and we learn by distinguishing one thing from another. A way to understand something is to consider its opposite. That is why we communicate in terms of hot or cold, good or bad, and up or down, especially when we are teaching new concepts to children.

There is, however, a downside to this type of interpretation. Black-and-white thinking

Balancing Worksheet

Read the statements below and answer yes or no

1. I think a lot about a situation and do very little about it. _____

2. I act spontaneously and get mixed results, which is frustrating. _____

3. I overreact and that gets me into trouble. _____

4. I suppress my true feelings. _____

5. I overeat when I am nervous, sad, or bored. _____

6. I usually forget to eat. _____

7. I find it hard to be understanding. _____

8. I don't enjoy learning new things. _____

9. I get bored with routine. _____

10. It's hard for me to find time for rest, nourishment, and enjoyment._____

11. I make impulsive decisions and then immediately want something else. _____

12. I am tired a lot. _____

13. I worry a lot. _____

14. I am angry a lot. _____

15. No one understands me. _____

16. I care for others more than I care for myself. _____

If another statement came to mind during this exercise, then add it to the list.

can cause you to "box in" certain experiences in your mind. For example, if you went on a hike once and did not enjoy it, you may think that you don't like hiking in general. But there may have been only a couple specific elements about the hike that you did not enjoy, which might be worth exploring further.

It is worth examining many types of general assumptions you may have. If you "hate to read," maybe you would enjoy books on tape. Or maybe you could reframe the way you think about reading, and instead of seeing it as boring you could see it as a way of learning interesting new things.

It is important for us to understand opposites. However, we must make sure to avoid stark contrasts, which narrow our thinking and limit our experiences.

Yin and Yang

The yin and yang symbol easily illustrates the basic philosophy that nothing is black or white. There is always a little of its opposite present. The concept allows for a softening in our belief structure and an ability to honor and respect what is different from our way of thinking. From here comes the knowledge, insight, and wisdom that can then bring about peace and harmony. This symbol is also used to represent Taoism (sometimes spelled Daoism), which is an ancient Chinese philosophy and religious tradition based on the *Tao Te Ching* that dates back two millennia. Eastern philosophies can easily be integrated into your life without disrespect to your own religious beliefs. The teachings are meant to provide guidance, as we all struggle to maneuver through life's challenges.

Everyday application of this principle is easy. Any time you look at a problem you will begin to see it isn't all bad. There is some good, hope, and possibility that is already waiting for you. The *Tao* teaches us that opportunity lies within the problem, and if you can see that, then you have something to work with. Have you ever heard someone come up with a good solution for a problem and then heard someone else say, "We've tried that and it doesn't work"? Next time this happens, encourage the person to provide more details. Understanding why it did not work is important. From here you can come up with a new solution. Simply discrediting an idea is seeing things as black and white.

To illustrate how easy it is to get stuck in a belief, imagine someone has sent you a photograph as an email attachment. You open up the picture and are struck by the beautiful rich red color of a single rose. If someone were to ask you to describe the picture, you would describe it as a red rose. But if you looked more closely at the color, at the individual pixels, you would see a variety of colors, like blue, green, and yellow. Together those colors make up the primary color your eyes recognize as red. There is often a rich variety of things hiding. Whatever you seek is already present, you just need to find it.

Let's explore further this concept of yin and yang. Below are some examples of characteristics that are either considered yin or yang.

You are missing the point if you use this information to make black-and-white assumptions about gender traits. This is a way to guide you through a mental exercise. Take each quality and look to its opposite for comparison purposes. Do you strongly identify with your female (or male) qualities and feel an imbalance in regards to how people relate to you? If so, consider what

Yin	Yang
Female	Male
Dark	Light
Inert	Active
Intuition	Intellect
Creative	Logical
Collaborative	Independent
Compassionate	Powerful
Right brain	Left brain

opposite qualities may be of value. A softer or stronger approach in your interactions with certain individuals may be helpful.

Right Brain and Left Brain

Do you like being a creative individual but find you lack structure in your life? Or maybe you have too much structure and no fun? There are two cerebral hemispheres to the brain, the left and the right. Some broad generalizations can be made about the unique functionality of the two hemispheres: The left hemisphere is the more logical side and the right is the creative side. People who are left-brained are more comfortable with habits and routines, while people who are right-brained are more comfortable with exploration and new behaviors.

EXERCISE 3.1

Close your eyes and imagine you are holding an apple. See the color of the apple and feel the texture. See all the details of your hand. Turn the apple slowly. Notice the light reflecting off the apple.

Determining Your Dominant Brain

Did you have a hard time seeing colors or movement during this exercise? Some people find it is difficult at first to visualize. If that is the case, it is likely you are left-brain dominant. Practice a bit and you will learn.

The right hemisphere of the brain controls the left side of the body and vice-versa. You can use this information when observing body language to determine someone's dominant hemisphere. This is useful information when communicating, because if the person is in the emotional right brain (maybe the left eyebrow is slightly lifted) then you can talk in terms of feelings instead of logic. An important note about body language is the eyes. If a person is looking to the left, they are engaging with the left brain—to recall information, for example. If the person is looking to the right they are accessing in their internal emotions or imagination.

Sometimes it is said that if a person is looking right they are lying. That is not always true. It could be that they are accessing newer information, thinking through something for the first time, or connecting with an emotion instead of a thought.

Shifting Your Dominant Brain

The dominant hemisphere shifts throughout the day, however most people have a preference for how they think about things. You can notice this with your breath. Place the back of your hand in front of your nostrils and notice if air is coming out of one side more than the other. If you are not congested, this could give you a clue to which side of the brain is currently dominant.

Some people prefer to use data to logically make decisions while others prefer to use intuition or emotions to make decisions. Understanding your preferences can help you to increase your awareness about how you and the people around you tend to operate. No way is right or wrong. But this understanding can help you to make conscious choices, which can then allow you to get better results. Remember—if you always do things the same way, you are probably going to continue to get the same results.

To consciously shift hemispheres, you can engage in certain activities. For example, you can do things like crosswords or problem solving puzzles to shift to the left. Knowing ways to shift can be useful when have a task you need to complete or an issue you need to resolve but don't feel like you are getting anywhere.

Let's say you cannot understand why someone is so upset with you. It could be you are currently left-brain dominate.

Take a moment to imagine something that makes you feel very happy, or try an artistic endeavor. Something like doodling can help you shift. Then reconsider the upset person's situation. Can you see it through their eyes? Can you begin to understand how an action, or lack thereof, has hurt the person? Can you come up with a peaceful resolution?

On the other hand, what if someone causes you to get emotional, but causes others to just roll their eyes. Work on a crossword puzzle and then reconsider the situation. See if your perspective changes. Maybe there are changes that you can begin to make that will allow you to interact better with that person but still honor your true self.

Using Ayurveda to Find Balance

Ayurveda Overview

Ayurveda is the sister science to Yoga philosophy, and therefore its origins date back at least two thousand years. It is based on the written texts known as the Vedas. Ayurveda is considered a form of alternative medicine in the United States. Treatment can range from simple techniques for self-care to complex treatments and procedures that are carried out by an Ayurvedic doctor or practitioner.

The Ayurveda system uses *doshas* to categorize things with similar biological characteristics. These groupings of similar characteristics offer us yet another guide to examine ourselves and alert us to an imbalance. If you are trying to find balance, it may be helpful to understand your dosha.

There are three doshas: *kapha*, *pitta*, and *vata*. Each dosha is comprised of two of the five elements, which in Ayurveda are air, space, fire, water, and earth. Note that the five elements of Ayurveda are different from those in Traditional Chinese Medicine. However, both systems serve to illustrate how things can be categorized and then used for bringing balance and harmony. Below is a brief description of each dosha with some examples of the biological characteristics or rhythms of nature for each.

Kapha: Earth and Water Elements

Examples of kapha are: areas of the body that are fluid based, the spring season, childhood, the time of day between six and ten (both a.m. and p.m.), and anything that is heavy or wet by nature. People are typically more kapha when they have a large bone structure. They have the greatest strength and endurance but move slower and can lack motivation. Kapha body types will tend to notice the most imbalances in the springtime. Kapha children tend to have more ear, nose, and throat problems because of their over-accumulation of fluids. Things with warm, drying qualities will bring balance to a kapha.

Pitta: Fire and Water Elements
Examples of pitta are: the digestive and metabolic systems in the body, the summer season, middle age, the time of day between ten and two (both a.m. and p.m.), and

anything that is hot or sharp by nature. People are typically more pitta when they have a medium bone structure. They also move quickly but can 'burn out' easily. They prefer cooler weather. Pitta body types will tend to notice more imbalances in the summertime. People between the age of twenty and seventy that have busy schedules tend to have an over-accumulation of pitta, and therefore things with grounding, cooling qualities will bring balance.

Vata: Space and Air Elements

Examples of vata are: the nervous system, the fall and winter seasons, old age, the time of day between two and six (both a.m. and p.m.), and anything light and dry by nature. People are typically more vata when they have small bone structure. They prefer to move quickly, and love to multitask. They also prefer warm weather. Seniors tend to feel colder because of changes in the circulatory system and they may notice more joint pain as well. Vata is the easiest dosha to imbalance because change in-and-of-itself is vata. Forgetfulness is another sign of vata imbalance. Things with kapha and pitta will help to bring balance.

If you are interested in learning what your dosha is, you can find references for quizzes you can take or you can see an Ayurvedic practitioner. However, if you do not choose to do further research but are interested in a high-level guide for bringing balance, you can refer to the tables below.

Using the Ayurveda Tables

Table One lists the three doshas, and includes a high-level summary of characteristics and signs or symptoms of imbalance. Even if you do not know your dosha, you can look at some of the signs and symptoms and see if they apply to you. If they do, then you may have an imbalance with that dosha, regardless of your primary dosha.

Once you know your dosha imbalance, you go to that row of Table Two for ideas on how to bring balance. The two columns are "Increase" and "Decrease." Follow these suggestions and you will notice improvements. Remember that Ayurveda is a detailed science, and the recommendations provided should be compared to any other self-care, like taking an aspirin for a headache. More complicated situations require professional medical care.

Balancing the Ayurveda Doshas

The concept behind balancing the doshas is easy. Too much of one quality causes an imbalance, so you need to seek out its opposite. For example, if you are a kapha dosha, you should not eat too many heavy, cold, oily, or sweet foods. If you do, you may start to feel heavy, depressed, tired, or gain weight. Instead, review the kapha balancing guidelines in Table Two and consider light, warm, and dry foods.

Here's another example: If you are normally a very passionate pitta dosha with a great enthusiasm, but you realize that your passion has turned to anger, then you've accumulated

Table I

Dosha	Characteristics	Signs/symptoms of imbalance
Kapha — Earth element (and some water), which is more prevalent in spring (and to some degree in winter) and in youth.	• Grounded and grounding for others • Confident • Steady, solid, strong • Consistent	• Tired, depressed, apathetic • Weight gain • Ear, nose, throat problems including colds, allergies, and asthma
Pitta — Fire element (and some water element), which is more prevalent in summer and in middle age.	• Great concentration, intelligent, good memory • Fun, passionate	• Extreme emotions (anger, jealousy, hatred, passion) • Judgmental and demanding • Heart and digestive problems
Vata - Air and space elements, which are most prevalent in fall and winter and in old age.	• Open to change • Flexible • Effective at multi-tasking	• Unable to make decisions • Detached, forgetful • Digestive, joint, and breathing problems • Dry skin, hair, etc.

Table II

	Consider	**Avoid**
Kapha	• Vigorous exercise • Light, dry, warming, and cooked foods • Bitter, astringent, and sour tastes • Spices	• Too much sleep • Heavy, cool, and oily foods • Sweet, salty, and sour tastes
Pitta	• Gentle exercise • Cool or warm foods and liquids • Sweet, bitter, and astringent tastes • Moderation	• Over heating or over doing it in general • Alcohol, tobacco, over eating • Hot spices and salty, sour, and pungent tastes
Vata	• Gentle exercise • Heavy, warm, and cooked foods • Sweet, salty, and sour tastes • Routine	• Too much change • Light, cold, dry, and raw foods; caffeine • Bitter, pungent, and astringent tastes (www.eattasteheal.com)

too much fire element and need some grounding and rest. Try following the pitta balancing guidelines in Table Two.

A vata imbalance can leave you feeling insecure or forgetful. Or you may notice your skin and hair are dry. Following the vata balancing recommendations in Table Two may help.

The purpose of sharing this information is to give you simple ideas that you can try on your own so that you can feel your best; however, the body is complex. You may think you have one particular imbalance based on a symptom such as feeling tired, and then think you need to follow the kapha balancing recommendations. In fact, you could have a vata imbalance that is "pushing kapha." In this situation, you should follow the vata balancing recommendations, which would encourage rest instead of activity.

For more information, you can refer to the references at the end of this book or work with an Ayurvedic practitioner. Just remember that if you are in a state of balance, then you will feel at ease and comfortable. Discomfort and dissatisfaction are signs of imbalance.

Balancing Your Diet with Ayurveda

Struggling with stress and any form of physical discomfort will lessen your chance for success with achieving your desires. You can improve how you feel by reducing stress and improving your diet and fitness levels. There are many options available, and using Ayurveda is one. If your success with other diets or programs has been disappointing then give these recommendations a try.

All the different diet options can be confusing, especially with so much conflicting information about things like calories, carbohydrates, proteins, and fats. Most products and programs have short-term results at best. The lack of sustainability suggests a problem with a fundamental belief as it relates to dieting. The word diet is thought to be a short-term approach to weight loss. Shifting that belief and redefining the word diet allows a person to begin to think of meaningful lifestyle change. Ayurveda offers an opportunity to get back to basics.

Ayurvedic practitioners do not identify "good foods" and "bad foods" the way many programs do. Claiming certain foods are "bad" can create an unhealthy relationship with food, and can also make you crave those foods more because you were just told not to have them. What do you think about when you are told not to eat ice cream? If you like ice cream, then you probably just visualized eating some. Willpower may help you avoid ice cream for some time. But when you finally do eat it, since you have been avoiding it, you will likely over-consume it.

While an Ayurvedic practitioner will give food recommendations to bring balance, he will not say a food is bad. Food is meant to be enjoyed. That enjoyable feeling, which diminishes stress, assists in the digestion process. However, the primary reason for consuming food is to bring necessary nutrients into your system. If your goal is to be healthy then consider enjoying foods that will also nourish the body.

Just like with the foods you consume, the concepts of Ayurveda do not indicate that you should engage in exercise you dislike. An Ayurvedic practitioner will recommend that your exercise leaves you feeling more energized instead of depleted.

Gunas and Balance

Everything has a natural evolutionary process. We are born, we live, and we die. Food is grown, harvested, and, if not consumed, rots. According to Sankhya and Vedantic philosophy, the *gunas* are the three intrinsic qualities of nature. Understanding the three gunas can help you to determine where you are at with life change. Are you stagnating or are you growing? Do you feel energized from your thoughts, foods, and activities, or do you feel burned out? Use the information below to help you to consider how you can bring balance. A summary of the energetic qualities for the three gunas are listed below.

Sattva: Purity
This includes fresh, clean thoughts and fresh, nourishing foods. This means foods that are fresh, light, sweet, juicy, nourishing, and give energy are sattva.

Rajas: Action
This includes motion, activity, and excitement. Rajasic foods are hot, dry, salty, sour, bitter, and pungent. Examples of rajas foods are spicy food, fried food, and anything consumed in excess.

Tamas: Inertia

This includes old, dry, distasteful, or dying things. Tamasic foods include all processed foods, including canned and frozen ones.

Both the doshas and gunas can help explain certain physiological and psychological characteristics. As illustrated in the descriptions above, you can see that Ayurveda also uses the three gunas to distinguish the foods we eat. When the foods you consume are fresh, it is easier to feel fresh. Sattvic foods take less energy to digest and leave you with energy for other things.

This can also happen with how you engage in thinking. If you continually feel angry or if you worry a lot, you will drag yourself down.

Instead, shift to positive thinking. As you learned with the yin and yang, every problem already has the solution. Focus on pure, calm thoughts and you will get better results; you are working with nature's growing process.

Here's an example: Have you ever had a conversation with someone that left you feeling emotional? Maybe he embarrassed you and left you angry at him. The conversation is over and you are at home now. But while you are physically at home, your mind is still back in the conversation, and you keep ruminating about it. Maybe you even call a friend and share the story with him. The more you engage in the thoughts and negative feelings, the worse you feel. You don't sleep well that night, and the next day is a disaster because you are tired. Now you are the one talking to others in an unkind way, and now maybe you have embarrassed or hurt someone else. You have an over-accumulation of excitement (raja) and emotion (pitta), and you should find balance through their opposites.

This type of mental punishment was a conscious choice and was totally of your own doing. The damage you have done to yourself (and maybe others) is worse than the initial situation. Instead, try next time to calm yourself down and then ask yourself what you can learn from the situation. If the person has treated you this way repeatedly, you may decide it is time to set a loving boundary with that person. Or you may consider that he may have been having a bad day and simply forgive and forget. Sometimes it's not about the other person at all. Any opportunity to learn something new about you creates room for positive change. The gunas aren't good or bad—they are part of the evolutionary process. Use them to your advantage.

EXERCISE 3.2:
Rumination

Think about a rumination (recurring thought) you have been having about yourself and determine if it is sattvic, rajasic, or tamasic. How can you shift the thought to feel clean, clear, fresh, or new? How can you bring about growth and positive change?

Nadis and Balance

In Traditional Chinese Medicine, *meridians* are energetic pathways that are used in modalities such as acupuncture. Unlike nerves, they cannot be seen and are considered part of our "soft anatomy" or "the subtle body." In Yogic teachings, meridians are known as nadis and there are over 72,000 of them. However, there are three main nadis: *ida*, *pingala*, and *sushumna*. The nadis connect to the central nervous system and have a direct impact on the health and wellbeing of the human organs. Yogis believe that when ida and pingala are balanced, a person can awaken *kundalini*, a type of inner power that leads to liberation—the ultimate life balance.

For our purposes, the importance of understanding the subtle body is to simply provide information that can be used to bring balance, wellness, and foster personal growth. Ida moves through the left nostril and is connected to the right brain and yin characteristics, while pingala moves through the right nostril and is connected to the left brain and yang characteristics. These nadis originate at the base of the spine, spiral up and down the spinal column, and end at the nostrils.

A breathing practice known as *nadi sodhana,* or alternate nostril breathing (see the exercise below), helps to bring balance to ida and pingala. This is helpful because most people have a tendency to think and behave in certain ways. Over time this can lead to imbalance.

If you are always very active and talkative, you may be overusing pingala and begin to notice symptoms that relate to excessive yang. This affects the hollow organs such as the stomach, intestines, or bladder. Common examples would be a stomach ulcer, heart burn, or any illness that is hot and sudden. If ida is overused then imbalances that relate to yin can occur, which includes solid organs such as the liver, spleen, pancreas, kidneys, heart, and lungs.

As a side note, the Sanskrit word *hatha* means sun (*ha*) and moon (*tha*). Ha refers to pingala and tha refers to ida. Hatha yoga refers to the physical aspects of the yoga practice, including *asanas* (postures) and *pranayama* (breathing techniques).

EXERCISE 3.3:
Nadi Sodhana -
Alternate Nostril Breathing Practice:

Step 1: *A* **mudra** *is a hand gesture. Traditionally, a gesture called the* **Vishnu Mudra** *is used to seal off one nostril.If this gets confusing, simply try to focus on the breathing piece.*

Technique: With your right hand, fold down the index and middle fingers and leave the thumb, ring, and pinky fingers open.When breathing through the right nostril (inhale and exhale), you keep the left nostril closed off with the ring and pinky fingers.When breathing through the left nostril, you can keep the right nostril closed using the thumb.

Step 2: *Each segment should be done for a count of four to eight.*

- *Close off left nostril and exhale through right nostril.*

- *Inhale through right nostril.*

- *Close off right nostril and exhale through left nostril.*

This breathing technique provides optimal function to both sides of the brain and is balancing, centering, and calming.

Chakras and Balance

Another aspect of the subtle body is the seven main chakras, or wheels of energy. These chakras run along the spinal column from the tail bone to the crown of the head. The ida and pingala nadis spiral around them. A brief description of the chakras will be provided below.

Why do the chakras matter when talking about life balance? Understanding how the chakras work and how to bring balance to them can help you to eliminate challenges from your life. Lack of information leaves people feeling helpless. New information can provide solutions. The overview in the table below is meant to provide information as it relates to life balance. For more information, refer to the resources listed at the end of this book.

CHAKRA DESCRIPTIONS

No.	English/ Sanskrit Name	Location	Functions
1	Root (Muladhara)	Base of spine	Safety, survival
2	Sacral (Svadisthana)	Abdomen	Emotions, relationships, creativity
3	Solar Plexus (Manipura)	Above navel	Personal power
4	Heart (Anahata)	Heart	Love, compassion
5	Throat (Visuddha)	Throat	Communication
6	Third Eye (Ajna)	Between eyebrows	Intuition
7	Crown (Sahasrara)	Crown of head	Union, Transcendence

Let's briefly examine each emotion by starting with the root chakra. If you feel fearful a lot of the time or tend to worry a lot, then you have a blockage in the first chakra that may be holding you back from enjoying life to its fullest. Obviously a real and immediate fear is something that should not be ignored, but here we are talking about worrying and mild phobias. For example, many people are afraid of public speaking. Or maybe you are fearful of flying, which causes extreme stress when you need to travel. In situations like these, addressing the problem to overcome the fear will be liberating and will make you feel safer because you no longer need to waste energy on this type of worry. Many times fear comes from a lack of experience, so practicing can make you feel better.

The second chakra is our pleasure center, which can create feelings of guilt. Cravings and addictions are a sign of imbalance here. Healthy life style choices can bring balance and a state feeling of confidence. Understanding the underlying needs as it relates to your cravings and satisfying them in a healthy manner is of utmost importance.

The third chakra is our personal power center. In this chakra, fear creates shame from the inability to stand up to others. This is different from the fears in the first chakra, which relate to safety. Building self-confidence comes from learning new things and then practicing them.

The first three chakras relate to your energy at a personal level. The next three express your energetic relationship to others and yourself.

The fourth chakra relates to love and sorrow. When in balance, you are a sympathetic, caring human being—not just for others, but also for yourself. A common imbalance is that some people are so giving that they forget to care for themselves. Then feelings of resentment and anger can start to occur. When life presents a difficult challenge, such as the loss of a loved one, deep sorrow is experienced. Grief is a heart-wrenching pain, but it is one that must be dealt with. To process something this large takes time and is essential to healing. Finding support groups or friends that you can openly talk with will help you to heal so that you can move forward again.

The fifth chakra relates to how you communicate with others and yourself. Are you honest with yourself? Or are you hiding behind stories that make you feel better? Self-deception is a form of lying, even though it can be hard to identify at first, because we really believe our own stories. You may think you are not doing something, like staying physically fit, because you are too busy—but deep down you know that you are lying to yourself. Being truthful cleanses the mind and heart and lets you live unburdened by the repercussions of your stories.

The sixth and seventh chakras are where higher truths can be uncovered. When your sixth chakra is balanced, your wisdom guides you and there is little struggle with the truth. It is easy to do what is right because you are no longer driven by your ego. The seventh chakra relates to spiritual development.

A chakra can be deficient or over-utilized, which can cause imbalance and impact other chakras. Here is an example: You are a loving, giving person. By always giving, you are over-utilizing the heart chakra in one way. This generally means you are not taking care of yourself. When you do not love yourself, you may begin to feel resentment and anger. This may also deplete your solar plexus, or third chakra, and will make you feel like you have no personal power. You will feel insecure.

Another common example of imbalance happens in the throat chakra. When we do not understand who we are, and instead identify strongly with our labels (like what you do for a living, or the things you own), we are not honestly communicating with ourselves or others. There is either a misalignment in communication, or you are relying on one-sided communication (always talking or always listening) too much.

Life situations can cause a constant shifting in your energetic balance. Again, the key ingredient to life balance is awareness of the imbalance.

EXERCISE 3.4

Now that you have read information about the chakras, do you see an area that is out of balance for you? Can you identify a positive change you can begin making?

Strength

With a clear understanding of what is desirable, you can now choose to move into an action phase. Action takes effort and even courage. When preparing for a physically challenging task, training helps to produce good results. Here your training will come from the exercises in this chapter.

// The biggest human temptation is to settle for too little. //

Thomas Merton

This chapter will help you to deepen your understanding of yourself and your desires. You will create a vision, which you can then use for your vision, mission, and purpose statements. These statements can be displayed in a location where you can see them each day to help you to stay on track. You will then set some goals and come up with a plan of execution. You will transition from an inner to an outer one. By the end of this chapter, you will be ready to move into action. Action, or lack thereof, both produce results. A well thought out plan increases your likelihood of success.

Awareness Before Action

Self-Affirmations

You have made a lot of progress. Learning more about yourself takes some effort, but hopefully you now feel more connected to your desires. We are going to work on creating a vision, but first let's take a moment to come up with a few brief self-affirmations. Repeating these will let you be your own cheerleader as you move forward. If you can also find friends and family to cheer you on, then that is even better. Think about the following ideas to get you ready for the exercise below: "I am a confident, loving person." "I know I deserve love." "I believe in myself."

EXERCISE 4.1:
Self-Affirmations

Write down a few self-affirmations in the space provided below.

Defining Your Success

How do you define success? It's an important question. If you are not sure, you may end up chasing someone else's dream. It is easy to buy into cultural or societal beliefs—but if you examine them more closely, you may realize some of those beliefs do not serve you well. So take time now before you begin to create your vision.

For example, it is fine if you are into status symbols, but it is just as important to understand why. Is it because you really want the Rolex or Lexus? Or are you sold on the idea by advertising? If you have the money in the bank and really want these things, then of course buy them and love them. But remember that these items alone do not make you successful. It's your character and personal attributes that make you successful. Avoid false labels that come from big purchases. Having nice things doesn't necessarily lead to happiness or success. And if you are buying things you cannot afford and are in debt, then you are probably not happy.

Think about defining success in a way that makes you feel the greatest sense of satisfaction. It may be more about relationships or health than material items. It's far more important to identify success from personal characteristics and values.

Finding an Anchor

When you want to incorporate a new behavior into your life, it can be easy to forget about it as you get busy with your day. Anchors can

EXERCISE 4.2:
My Definition of Success

Briefly describe your personal definition of success in the space provided below.

hold you in place and keep you from drifting. If you are the type of person who finds that your logical left brain gets in the way of being open and compassionate to others, or if your right-brain dominance is hindering your ability to think about situations with logic versus emotion, then come up with an anchor. You have to start somewhere, and if you continue to forget to exhibit a new behavior, it can seem like you just can't do it. Yes you can; you just need practice.

Remember, first you need the desire to try something new and then you need to believe you can do it. The anchor will remind you to do it. An anchor allows you to connect to something factual. It can be an accomplishment of your own or someone else's. An anchor may be a role-model you have identified. Or it could be a visual reminder, like a note on the refrigerator. You could even give that old string-wrapped-around-your-finger technique a try.

EXERCISE 4.3:
Creating a Role Model

- *Think about someone you admire and why.*

- *Write down the ways you imagine that person would act in everyday situations.*

- *Select ideas you want to include and use that string if necessary.*

The Vision

Now that you have a heightened level of
self-awareness, you are ready to articulate
your vision. Your vision is much more than
your goals. Below are some suggestions to
consider when creating your vision:

- **Use your imagination.** Activate your
  creative right brain and don't let your
  logical left brain tell you a dream is too
  big. See your life in its entirety, as you
  want it to be. Include your ideal home,
  relationships, and career. Imagine how
  you would look and feel. Not only will
  this make you feel good, but you are
  also completing the puzzle of your
  identity in your mind's eye. You can
  see how everything can fit together
  perfectly.

- **Be specific.** Without details, it's hard to know what steps to take first in achieving your goals. You can waste your time and money, and that's discouraging. Different people can have the same goal, but if their visions are different then they will probably take a different course of action. Say the goal is financial security. That's a very vague goal, without knowing anything else about your interests and desires. To achieve financial security, one might: go to college to learn skills for a great job, become an entrepreneur, go on an adventure that leads to a discovery and monetary reward, or marry well. The goal is the same, but the paths to achieving it are entirely different because of the visions.

- **Look at yourself from the outside.** Have you ever heard the saying "it's hard to see the forest through the trees"? Sometimes you need to get out of the forest to a higher vantage point to take in the full view. Each tree represents an aspect of your life: an intention, goal, responsibility, challenge, behavior, hobby, or personality trait. Getting out of the forest and observing your own life from the hilltop can give breathtaking perspective.

- **Get excited about the journey.** Have you ever planned a trip and enjoyed thinking about it prior to your departure? Of course you have. That's half the fun. Don't look at the journey as cumbersome—realize how exciting it's going to be.

EXERCISE 4.4:
Creating a Vision

- *Get comfortable and close your eyes.*

- *Begin to imagine each aspect of your life as you truly wish it to be. Don't settle or use logic. Dream big.*

- *See in your mind's eye how it can all fit together. Are there any contradictions? Can you see a way around them? If you can make sense of it in your head, then you can begin turn your dream into reality.*

Remember that this is your vision right now. Visions can change over time. If you want, make this part of your daily practice.

Sharpen the Vision

Try these simple tips when using your mind's eye to see your vision:

- See the image as if you are watching it through your own eyes. If you see yourself in a big, fancy office, imagine looking at your hands touching the grain of the wood on your desk or seeing a beautiful view out of your office window.

- See the images in color and close up. If the image is far away or in black and white, then you are not making your vision realistic. You want your mind to believe the images to be real.

- See the image in real time and not like a still photograph.

- Use all your senses. If you are imagining you are in a cafe in Italy, then notice the smells, tastes, and sounds.

- Enjoy the feelings that come from your vision.

At the very least, your visualization should leave you feeling great. You are aligning your energy with your desires. This increases the likelihood of success. Now it's time to create a vision, mission, and purpose statement.

Vision, Mission, and Purpose Statements

Drafting a Vision Statement

Have you ever looked at an amazing view and felt so calm and peaceful? Your vision statement can evoke those feelings. A vision statement is your opportunity to clearly articulate your big picture. Remember not to analyze or judge your thoughts. Write from your heart. It doesn't need to be realistic; it shouldn't be. Never aim too low. Your vision does not need to be limited to yourself.

EXERCISE 4.5:
Draft a Vision Statement

- *Write down as much as you'd like about what came to mind during the previous exercises on a separate sheet of paper. Include thoughts and feelings.*

- *Review what you have written down. Are there any major themes? If so, jot those down as well.*

- *Draft one sentence per major theme in the space provided below*

Clearly Stating Your Vision

Can you sum up what you wrote in Exercise 4.5 into a few words or sentences? If you pick something short and easy to remember, then you can repeat it to yourself throughout the day as a reminder to align your actions with your vision. Acting in alignment with your vision brings greater success.

EXERCISE 4.6:
My Vision Statement

Write your vision statement below.

Knowing your vision statement will allow you to make sure all of your actions are in alignment with it. Any actions that are not in alignment with your vision can be analyzed. Why do you do these things? Responsibilities, commitments, core values, and needs are a few possibilities. Go through each one and make a conscious choice on each of these actions. Then determine if there are ways you can either include them in your vision or set some loving boundaries.

Purpose Statement

Your purpose statement is your attempt to answer the biggest questions of all. Who are you? Why are you here? This is a great time to reflect on the ideas of "identity" and "core values" that you explored earlier in this book. Your purpose may be to be a great parent or good provider. Your purpose may be to provide things like comfort, beauty, humor, or protection for others. Your purpose may be to deepen your spiritual connection or to save the planet. Or maybe your purpose is to follow your vision and mission. Your purpose can and probably will change throughout your life, and it is a great thing to consider, because it will help you find your true path and follow it.

EXERCISE 4.7:
My Purpose Statement

Write your purpose statement below.

Mission Statement

Your mission speaks to how you will achieve your vision and purpose. Ask yourself *how* you will accomplish your vision and purpose. This begins to lead you into goal setting, but differs from that because these are big goals that will be ongoing.

EXERCISE 4.8:
My Mission Statement

Write your purpose statement below.

Setting Goals to Realize Your Vision

Two steps for good decision making

Typically you will have a positive feeling related to a thought when that thought is in agreement with your values and beliefs. Conversely, you will typically have a negative feeling when a thought is not in agreement with your values and beliefs. Sometimes a thought will create no feeling, which is an indicator that you have no awareness or attachment. You can see a sunrise and be overwhelmed with joy, but if you are preoccupied or uninterested you may feel nothing. Your present state of mind has a lot to do with affecting an outcome.

Now that you are ready for action, consider using these two steps to help you make good decisions:

1)   Stay connected with your vision, mission, and purpose statements. Print them out and, if possible, memorize them. These statements are your benchmarks, which will establish your standards for decision making. Are your desired actions in alignment with your vision, mission, and purpose statements? If so, then you are living in integrity with your true self and making the correct decision.

2)   You must practice awareness so you do not miss opportunities that you may otherwise miss when you are preoccupied. This almost always occurs when the mind is wandering. Let's use the sunrise example again. Have you ever been so lost in thought

that someone else will ask you if you saw a sunrise or rainbow and you realize you did not? We are often preoccupied when we are overwhelmed or stressed out. Too many activities or commitments in your life will make it more challenging for you to experience real transformation. Your clearer understanding of your true self, and greater awareness to where you are and how you are living your life, will allow you to make enriching life choices. You can still honor your commitments. But you should evaluate why you have all of those responsibilities. Your increased awareness will allow you to make the distinctions and the changes required.

Goal Setting and the Strategizing Worksheet

Now you are finally ready to set some goals. It can be tempting to jump in and begin making a lot of changes, but taking time to prioritize and plan will help you get better results. In my first book, *Four Steps to a Better Life*, I provided a Strategizing Worksheet that is also included at the end of this section. Here are some general guidelines you can follow.

1. **Use good goal-wording.** If your goal sounds like a chore or has the words 'should' or 'need to' in it, then you will have a hard time getting good results. "I need to lose weight" or "I should spend more time with my family" are good examples of poor goal-wording. Take a moment to think about what it

is that you want. "Losing weight" is not a well-defined goal because it doesn't explain why. State clearly your desired outcomes. Do you want to look good or to fit into your favorite jeans? Do you want to have more energy to have fun with your kids or quality time with your spouse? These are examples of good goal-wording.

Also, do not include the words "I wish" at the beginning of your goal. Just leave those words out and keep the remainder of your sentence.

2.   **Avoid limiting beliefs.** Limiting beliefs are things like, "I can't because my wife won't let me," or, "I'm not creative enough." Beliefs that support

your goal must be in place first. If you want a big promotion at work then you need to think about the qualities that will get you in that position, not the reasons you shouldn't be there. Listen to your inner monologue or how you talk to others. If you hear yourself say "I can't," then pay attention. Identify the limiting belief and come up with a replacement that will support your endeavors.

Let's illustrate this using the "recession" example. Does a recession mean you cannot be prosperous? Examine that belief statement. If someone can be prosperous during a recession then you can be too. Don't trap yourself with these types of beliefs.

3. **Identify your resources.** You cannot expect to be successful if an unexpected setback happens. Try to prepare yourself by taking some time to think about the resources you will need. If you do not have access to those resources, then consider how you can obtain them. This may require setting your main goal aside for a while and creating a preliminary goal first. Don't let that discourage you. Remember to enjoy the journey.

4. **Identify your support system.** Don't reinvent the wheel and waste time with tasks that you do not enjoy or understand; find people that are good at those tasks to help you whenever possible. Most importantly, try to

spend more time with like-minded individuals. Create a mastermind group. A mastermind group consists of at least one other individual who has similar goals. Together you can challenge each other to stay on the path. This person can help motivate you when you start to lose energy and focus. Join groups and clubs. Consider hiring a life coach, or ask your family and friends to hold you accountable.

5. **Create action items**. There are two types of action items. The first kind is an item that you can accomplish and check off your list. These types will have a completion date. Consider writing not only this date in your calendar but some ongoing reminders so that you

meet your deadline. The second type of action item is an ongoing task. If you do not want to let your bills pile up on your desk, then have an ongoing action item to go through your mail each evening. This is another way of creating a good habit.

STRATEGIZING WORKSHEET

1) Develop and Prioritize Goals	Short term goals (less than three months):
	Long term goal:
2) Understand Your Situation	List your values specific to goal:
	List your beliefs specific to goal:
	List key behaviors related to your goal:
	Do you have the time to dedicate to your goal?
	Are there any pitfalls or downside to your goals?
	What other changes are required of you or others?
	Other obligations/commitments that may interfere?
3) Identify Resources	What resources are needed and available?
	What resources are not available and how could you get them?

STRATEGIZING WORKSHEET
(Continued)

4) Create a Support System	Individuals: Groups:

5) Assign Measurable Action Items and Completion Date	Action Item	Completion Date
	1)	
	2)	
	3)	
	4)	

Establishing a Practice

There are many good reasons to establish a practice and some of them will be mentioned below. But what is a practice? The American Heritage Dictionary defines a practice as "to do or perform habitually or customarily; make a habit."

A person who makes a conscious decision to do something, rain or shine, happy or sad, learns how to overcome excuses that can hold them back from advancement. It's easy to come up with a dozen reasons why not to do something. That is why few people really excel with their goals. People with great athletic, musical, and spiritual desires all have a practice. Yoga is a practice. It's the act of repetition and dedication that gets the results. It takes dedication to excel. Here are some things to keep in mind as you establish your practice.

1. **Behaviors:** It is your actions alone that will get you results. If you want to fit into your favorite jeans, then you can't eat a bowl of ice cream every evening. But don't just think of a list of behaviors you want to stop— nature abhors a vacuum, so think of a productive behavior to replace it. Instead of ice cream, consider drinking herbal tea to help you to feel full or go for a walk to eliminate boredom.

2. **Habits:** Have you ever been so entrenched in thought that all of a sudden you realize you have reached your destination without even knowing it? You are so used to the

act of driving or walking that it requires no conscious thought. What other actions do you do without even thinking about them?

Habits are these types of thoughtless behaviors. That's great if your habits are good, but bad news if your behavior does not support your goal. You may need to make some changes that will help alert you of these habits, like finding an anchor.

3. **Needs:** It is important to talk about needs; some habits are extra hard to break because we are trying to satisfy a need. We have basic needs, like food and water, however we also have lots of emotional needs. Some people thrive on attention while others

need to feel a sense of belonging. Like our basic physical needs, the drive to fulfill emotional needs can override any other desires. The stronger the need, the more your attention is focused on satisfying the need. If you find you are having a hard time achieving a goal, it could be that you have an underlying unmet need. Maybe you want to lose weight, but your need for comfort is stronger. If ice cream at night makes you feel comfortable, and therefore satisfies this need, then it will be hard to overcome the urge to eat it. The only way you will move forward is to identify the need and find a better way of satisfying it.

With these things in mind, commit to creating a practice so you can manifest the changes you desire. Use this book to establish a practice. With it you will create good behaviors and habits, and more of your needs will be met by productive and positive means. Your discipline and commitment will help you to gain confidence and ease. You will learn more about yourself and your world.

YEN PATH WORKSHEET #2:
MY PRACTICE

Date:_____

Having a practice creates good habits. Through positive thought and action you will move closer to your desires. As you read the book, select techniques that will add to your practice.

My daily practice will include	Action item	When (day/time)
Practice non-judgment and not complaining (example)	Take a deep breath instead	Ongoing
Practice meditating (example)	Sit for 5 minutes a day on deck	7 a.m. daily
1.		
2.		
3.		
4.		

My weekly practice	Action item	When (day/time)
Practice not complaining	Guided visualization	Sunday evening
Set an intention (example)	Write it down	Monday morning
1.		
2.		
3.		
4.		

My quarterly practice	Action item	When (day/time)
Create a role model (example)	Write it down	First Saturday of season
Strategizing Worksheet (example)	Fill out the form	First Saturday of season
1.		
2.		
3.		
4.		

Appendix: The Practice Menu of Options

CHAPTER - 5

Stretch

Up until now, you have learned to gain clarity around your desires by centering and finding balance, and how to get good results through preparation and action. You may want to pause here and try these new skills out for a while. However, if you find you are still not getting the results you desire, or if you are simply a person that is always ready to learn more, then this will be the chapter for you.

I want to stress that I do not believe these ideas to be a definitive answer to life's problems. These ideas are only meant to enhance other belief systems and modes of support. If you are not getting what you need, or you are really struggling, I encourage you to explore other ways of getting perspective and support. For example, you could consider Cognitive Behavior Therapy (CBT), which "focuses on the here-and-now cause of your problems: your irrational self-talk. Numerous studies support the efficacy of this approach for a wide range of problems: anxiety, depression, procrastination, relationship problems, and addictions."

"The empires of the future are empires of the mind."

Winston Churchill

Read what follows with an open mind to see if these theories can help you realize the potential of positive thought. Here you may stretch or expand your beliefs. Just as physical stretching creates length in the muscle, mobility in the joints, and greater ease of movement, so does mental stretching. You will begin to notice a sense of freedom through the new options that you never considered before. This can open new doors; the more you learn, the more likely you will create positive change. If you'd like, find other sources of information on your own. Here is your opportunity to stretch, expand, and grow.

You will learn about three concepts in this chapter. The first concept illustrates how you can use your biological energy more efficiently with mind/body connection practices. You may find this helpful if you are the type of person that always thinks about things other than the present moment, or if you tend to feel negative and unhappy. You will also find this chapter helpful if you want scientific proof that positive thinking does make a real difference.

The second concept defines the universal laws of attraction, action, polarity, relativity, rhythm, cause and effect, and gender. Whether or not you believe in or even know about these laws does not matter. These concepts can apply to everything, and you may find that this information will help you gain new perspective on situations in your life.

The third and last concept in this chapter will be a brief overview of quantum mechanics and how it relates to you and the results you get in life. To fulfill your desires, you must align your perceptions, beliefs, and actions. Hopefully these theories will provide the exact pieces to the puzzle you have been looking for.

The First Stretch: Biological Energy and "The New Biology"

Scientific discoveries can lead to new areas of focus, or "new science." One example is in biology. On July 24, 2007, *NOVA* aired a show on PBS about Epigenetics, and describes the topic as follows: "Now it appears that our diets and lifestyles can change the expression of our genes. How? By influencing a network of chemical switches within our cells collectively known as the epigenome."

Epigenetics refers to a genetic expression that happens because of something outside of the gene, even though the DNA itself does not change. The concept has interesting implications for how we might view the inevitability of certain diseases. Is someone predisposed to obesity obese because they accepted this fate? Instead of assuming you will get sick, can you assume you will not? Is it possible that way of thinking might have real life results?

Many stories have been told of people miraculously recovering from an untreatable disease or learning to walk again after a terrible accident. While these "miracles" or outliers may be the exception, they are still worthy of examination.

During Bruce Lipton's talk in Seattle Washington in October 2009, he told the story of a family that knew they had a genetic predisposition to certain disease. Lipton goes on to state that DNA testing of the family showed that some family members without the gene still developed the disease, simply because they believed it would happen. One family member may do all they can to live a healthy life and not get the disease, while others may succumb to what they belief is the inevitable.

Another example of a "new science" is Signal Transduction Science. Lipton states in his book *The Biology of Belief* that, "[Signal Transduction Science]reveals a new awareness that our genes are constantly being remodeled in response to life experience." Previously, scientists believed that our genetics determined our outcomes. Now many scientists believe another important factor in gene expression is how the brain interprets information. This is because the brain releases chemicals into the blood stream based on this interpretation, which then alters the body's environment and subsequently influences gene expression.

New science is allowing for the important mind/body connection. If a person believes they can heal, then the opportunity is there for them. When confronted with a negative change or situation in your life, it is natural to feel sadness, loss, and fear. However, it is possible to move beyond grief and begin to feel emotions associated with a positive outcome. Yes, you must digest, process, and assimilate challenging occurrences. However, sometimes you can create a bad habit by living with the fear, sadness, or worry. Yoga teaches us to move from the extreme emotions to a place that is calming and centering. If you'd like, refer back to the earlier chapters and use some of the practices. From a calm, centered place you can regroup and take control. You can begin to implement changes to foster growth and healing.

For now, it is simply important to consider the possibilities for yourself. Do you tend to focus on a label like "I have _____," which is the name of a disease, illness, or lack of something like money? Or can you shift your focus to a positive, healthy label instead? Think of the opportunity, not the challenge, and you will attract what you want in life. And please take the time to see the beauty around you.

Dr. Dean Ornish has been a leader in promoting holistic health and is best known for helping patients reverse heart disease through lifestyle changes. He believes a healthy life style can affect a person at a genetic level: "If you live healthy, eat better, exercise, and love more, your brain cells actually increase." This approach to life will help you to feel your best so you can focus on your greater achievements. He says, "your genes are not your fate."

EXERCISE 5.1

Pick something in your life you are struggling with and identify where your focus lies in that area. How can you begin to shift your focus?

The Second Stretch: Universal Laws

The universe has order and is predictable if you learn to understand the rules. Everything in nature works in alignment with these laws. This section will allow you to acquaint yourself with some of these universal, or metaphysical, laws and help you explore how you can begin to work with the forces of nature. The laws work regardless of your perception or knowledge of them. The reason people get frustrated and struggle with change is because of resistance to these laws. These laws will help you to find balance and harmony, which will eliminate frustration and struggle.

Law of Attraction

This law gained a lot of popularity from the movie and book called *The Secret*. This universal law will provide you with what it is you think about. If you think about being in debt, then that is what you will attract. In other words, it is not likely that you will be prosperous when you think about debt all the time.

In actuality, it's not thinking about debt that causes it. However, the feelings associated with that thought generate the attraction. This means that you must not only think about prosperity, but also feel the feelings associated with prosperity if you want to attract it. How would you feel if you were prosperous? What would your life look like? Focus on that.

At first it may seem odd, but understand that you have simply created a bad habit by focusing on something negative. The thoughts and feelings must shift first. Visualize abundance and feel the joy and happiness move through you. Believe in your heart that you can bring about the changes you desire.

Focusing your thoughts and feelings on what you want to attract will allow you to see opportunities you would not have seen otherwise.

EXERCISE 5.2

Visualize something you wish to have an abundance of in your life. See yourself already living the life with this abundance by using the techniques you have learned. Enjoy the positive feelings from this practice.

Law of Action

Action is everything—you must choose different actions based on the identification of possibilities. If you want to be healthy, then practice your visualizations and feel the healing occurring. But also move forward from that practice with actions that are in alignment with your desire.

The law of attraction is an important step towards success, but you must engage in actions to support your desires. The only way to manifest your dreams and desires is to act upon them.

EXERCISE 5.3

What is it that you really want? What action can you take in order to create this possibility?

Law of Polarity

Everything has poles, or opposites. Without one you cannot experience the other. You cannot have cold without hot or love without hate. Have you ever had a bad headache and then noticed how good you felt when it was gone? Living in the extremes is rarely comfortable, and most people want to gravitate towards the center. That's why people fear change, because the awareness of the differences is now present and that makes them uncomfortable. It is foreign. However, as we are learning, sometimes change is just what is needed. After a while, the intensity of the change diminishes and we can then again find center.

EXERCISE 5.4

You may be tempted to stay with a negative thought. First determine if there is some knowledge you can gain. If so, make the appropriate changes. Otherwise consider the negative thought as simply a bad habit and make a conscious choice to focus on the opposite pole.

Law of Relativity

We tend to label things as good or bad, which is an example of polarity but in reality there is an entire spectrum in the middle. You may think your life is challenging, but then if you listen to other people or watch the news, you may realize you don't have it so bad. For example, two people can lose their job. One will have a positive attitude and begin a job search or maybe start a new business. One will feel depressed and unmotivated and will have a greater likelihood of remaining unemployed. This is the law of relativity. With this law, we can compare our life situations to others that are worse to feel thankful. We can also acknowledge others that are doing better to help ourselves establish new goals.

EXERCISE 5.5

Think of a situation that was a struggle in your life, and then compare that to similar struggles that other people have overcome. Learn how to make positive change from your struggles and be grateful for your blessings.

Law of Rhythm

Everything has a cycle and flows either in and out or up and down. The sun and moon rise and set, the tides come in and go out, and the seasons change. You too will experience cycles. Sometimes that means you will feel unproductive. Use these opportunities to rest or to catch up on other things instead. You will experience difficult times even if you do practice positive thoughts and actions. This is known as the law of rhythm. Know that these too will pass.

"How people treat you is their karma; how you react is yours."

Wayne Dyer

EXERCISE 5.6

When life does not go as planned, it is easy to try to push to get results. Consider being a receiver instead. Take a moment to practice a breathing exercise from the previous chapters. If you take time to be still, you may find you feel more relaxed and better able to assess your situation. Try moving in another direction or rest and wait it out.

Law of Cause and Effect

This is the relationship between events. Newton's law of motion states that "to every action there is always an equal and opposite reaction." Therefore, nothing happens by chance and everything is a result of a previous occurrence.

Another word for this law is *karma*. We will "reap what we sow." Every hardship and blessing has come to you for a reason, whether you know what that reason is or not. When you think of things in these terms, you can reflect back to see if you can discover a reason for a hardship so you can learn from it and make a positive change going forward. But sometimes bad things seem to happen to good people. Since we are all interconnected, it could be that the hardship or blessing is a result of someone else's karma. Don't worry about the past. Learn from it and move on.

Understanding this law can help you to see the importance of each and every one of your actions. Thoughtful action with good intention will create a positive effect.

Law of Gender

> **EXERCISE 5.7**
>
> *Reflect on a situation and find the lesson and the blessing. Be grateful for both and move forward with thoughtful awareness of your actions.*

The yin and yang principles are the basis for all of creation. If you would like, refer back to Chapter Three to remind yourself of these teachings. If you want to create, then you must find balance between these two forces. To be in balance, you must work and play, give and take. Let your feelings guide you and whenever possible seek balance.

The Third Stretch: Quantum Mechanics

Quantum mechanics describes many phenomena that did not adhere to Newtonian physics. Science proves that thoughts (waves or non-matter) become things (matter). Scientists explore how they are connected. Great consideration has been given to the topic of how thoughts impact us and our surrounding environment. Alan Sokal, a physics professor at NYU, writes:

> *Bell's theorem and its recent generalizations show that an act of observation here and now can affect not only the object being observed —as Heisenberg told us—but also an object arbitrarily far away (say, on Andromeda galaxy). This phenomenon — which Einstein termed ``spooky" — imposes a radical reevaluation of the traditional mechanistic concepts of space, object and causality, and suggests an alternative*

worldview in which the universe is characterized by interconnectedness and (w)holism: what physicist David Bohm has called ``implicate order."

EXERCISE 5.8

In what ways are you currently out of balance? Remember that it can change from moment to moment. Your awareness will allow you to determine the appropriate changes.

This matters because it can reframe how you think. If you understand the importance of each and every thought, then you may want to start to create more positive thoughts. This may become a very important point as it relates to your success and the success of those around you. It requires each of us to hold ourselves to a higher standard, because if we are really just a piece of the whole, then the only way we will flourish is if those around us do. This is easy to understand when we think in terms of our bodies. If you are sick, it is hard to function well. You become consumed with simply getting better. The same is true for our planet and beyond. If any piece of the whole is sick, then we all suffer.

Our society seems to thrive on negative information. With technology that allows us to see "news" from around the world, we are inundated with horrifying and sad images. These images make us angry, and we learn it is OK to judge and fight others, even if it is for a seemly good cause. Negativity and judgment are like cancer cells devouring healthy cells. A negative mindset simply creates more negativity and further divides and destroys. The sooner we realize that all of us on this planet will live and die together, the sooner we can begin to implement real change.

So what do you do if you strongly disagree with someone else's viewpoint? Do we need to fight? Perhaps we can resolve differences by realizing we all want the same thing, which is a peaceful existence that allows everyone and everything to flourish.

Of course as living entities we do feel pain and want to avoid that. We are sad at times and deeply grieve our losses. There is unspeakable suffering in the world that is beyond the control of one person, and so many big issues that cannot be resolved here. However, if you want positive change, you need to consider what energetic connection you are putting behind your thoughts and actions. Actions that come from the heart and mean no harm create good karma. The person that cuts another to cause harm or personal gain will experience bad karma in return.

If you increase your awareness through observation and learning, you will gain insight and wisdom. This will allow you to create wholeness in your life and in the world around you.

The Quantum Body

Now we will shift our focus from the big picture to what's going on inside the human body. As mentioned earlier, negativity is like a cancer that is destroying everything in its path. This has major implications as it relates to the health and wellbeing of your body. If you strongly connect to negative feelings on a regular basis, realize it is a bad habit you can break. It is normal to have bad feelings when something bad happens. But you can move beyond that if you choose.

There are trillions of cells in the human body, and as you learned earlier in this chapter, your biology is directly impacted by the feelings associated with your thoughts. Chronic negativity will make you sick. For example, chronically angry people are more likely to get heart disease and chronically sad people suffer from depression. Negative and sad emotions increase the likelihood of obesity and alcoholism. While life can be challenging, your perceptions and beliefs are always your choice. You can choose to change and lead a better life. You can choose to fulfill your desires.

Fortunately, we are replacing old cells with new ones all the time. This creates an amazing opportunity, because if you are creating new cells then you can create healthy ones— and increasing your awareness is how you begin that process. As we covered earlier, everything has a level of consciousness. Now that you are aware of that, you can make new strides.

In Deepak Chopra's book *Perfect Health: The Complete Mind/Body Guide*, he explains how to live in tune with your quantum mechanical body. To paraphrase, he suggests that you can activate the full potential of your quantum mechanical body with a few processes that come under your control every day. These processes are eating healthy foods, digestion, elimination, and correct breathing practices. All of these topics are covered in his book.

The way you take care of your body and mind are crucial in your success. It will be much easier to fulfill your desires if you have the energy to do so.

Relax

The Final Exercise

At the end of every yoga practice the student gets to rest, and so this book will end in the same way. You have learned a lot and have done a lot of work relating this knowledge to your own life. Now we will close with one final practice—the practice of showing respect and gratitude.

The remainder of this chapter is dedicated to real-life success stories of people that have changed their lives through either yoga or life coaching.

FINAL EXERCISE:
Namaste

Namaste *literally means "I bow you."*
Yoga classes end with this word exchanged
between teacher and students. Take a
moment to close your eyes. If you'd like,
you can bring your palms together at
heart center (in yoga this is the **Anjali**
Mudra—*the salutation seal) and bow your*
head. Now take a moment to focus on your
breath. Honor yourself and all the good
that you do. Then honor others you are
grateful for.

I hope you have found *Yen Path* to be clear and meaningful. I want to thank you for choosing this journey and wish you all the best. Namaste.

Success Stories

I am a very big yoga enthusiast and practicing yoga has been a lifesaver for me. I am a survivor of a severe brain stem injury, which also severely injured my cerebellum (which controls balance) and yoga helps me to manage my lack of equilibrium and to reduce stress, which is something that makes my vertigo worse.

I also wrote a book called Go Back and Be Happy, and I briefly mention how yoga has been a great help in my recovery. As a person who has been an athlete her entire life, and who was recently able to complete my first triathlon after my injury, I can really speak to how beneficial yoga is!

Julie Papievis
www.GoBackandBeHappy.com

I used to laugh at people who did yoga. I had a heart attack at age 45; I was in great shape at the time, but had very high cholesterol. I have changed a lot in my life since then. One key—yoga. It wiped me out, but I loved it. I remember the very first session. It was the longest hour of my life. Of course, it was a ninety-minute practice, so that was part of it.

Also, I remember seeing a skinny girl in her teens next to me, and I was thinking, "I've got to be way stronger than her." Wrong! She smoked through the class doing every advanced move while I was sucking air in down dog. But needless to say, I went back a week later, and from then on, I was hooked.

I now like it for both the physical and mental aspects. I wish I had tried it twenty years ago. But I guess better late than never.

Brian Hemsworth

I went to a weeklong workshop that changed me profoundly and put the wheels in motion for a massive change in my life. I met my real self for the first time—which, for a previously hardened and cynical person, was life-altering. I ended up leaving my job of seventeen years soon thereafter; I also found a completely new way of authentically being with my loved ones and others.

Bruce Irving

I have used life coaching and been able to surpass my goals more than I expected, delivering strong results for myself and employees, with my energy and ability to influence them to be at their best level. In return this resulted in extreme profits for the employer and for the staff. I helped many double their paychecks and a few even quadrupled, by showing them they didn't have to take no for an answer.

Rudy

I was diagnosed with bipolar disorder when I was 30 years old. Yoga is one of the ways I keep myself balanced, happy, productive, and healthy.

Anonymous

Index

Exercises